THE
Mis-Education
of the Masses

What they didn't teach you at school

WAYNE MALCOLM

MINISTRY IN ART PUBLISHING
communicating excellence

Ministry In Art Publishing Ltd
email publishing@ministryinart.com
www.miapublishing.com

This publication is designed to provide accurate and authoritative
information in regard to the subject matter covered. It is sold with
understanding that the publisher is not engaged in rendering legal,
accounting, or other professional service. If legal advice or other expert
assistance is required, the services of a competent professional
should be sought.

ISBN: 978-0-9551496-9-6

Cover design & layout by David Springer

Table of contents:

Foreword

In an age of accelerated change, overwhelming complexity and tremendous competition, we need leadership we can count on and **'out of the box'** thinking that will give us the mindset and skill set to navigate the volatile and turbulent times in which we live.

Bishop Wayne Malcolm is an International resource to whom corporations and individuals turn for mind set transformation and break-through strategies. In this ground breaking work, Bishop Malcolm provides a step by step process of what is required to change one's personal and professional mental blueprint.

You will find each chapter of this book challenging you to get outside of your comfort zone and inspire you to take charge of your life and create a new future.

His profound insight and cutting edge approach, gained from years of pastoring, counseling and lecturing, has earned him National and international acclaim.

As an entrepreneur and business coach Bishop Malcolm's experiential training workshops have transformed and motivated thousands of entrepreneurs, business leaders and their teams at all levels. This book is designed to teach you how to bring out the best in yourself and others. His approach and mind-set strategies will stretch your mind, touch your heart and dramatically expand the impact of your life.

I suggest that you use this book as a tool to carve out a life of purpose and meaning and at the same time create value and impact for others. If you are ready to change your life, increase your wealth and be all that God intended you to be, fasten your seat belt and get ready to **soar.**

Les Brown

Author, *"Live Your Dreams"* and
'It's Not Over Until You Win"
Motivational Speaker and Speech coach

www.thehomebusinessacademy.com

Dedication

Although many mentors and teachers have contributed to my understanding of this subject, I would like to pay tribute to the late Carter G Woodson (1875-1950). His masterpiece book entitled, **'The Mis-Education of the Negro'** fell into my hands several years ago and with it fell the missing pieces of a generational puzzle. Woodson's experience as an educator was vast; teaching and lecturing over several decades, on many continents to diverse ethnicities, he gained a bird's-eye view of educational systems around the world.

His book does not seek to knock educators or to undermine educational institutions. Instead he makes an observation concerning the way that Negroes were educated after the civil war. He noted that their own history was omitted from most curriculums and that their sense of inferiority was often re-enforced by their education. He further noted that nothing in their learning enabled them to make a living or to achieve success. He drew a distinction between being un-educated and being mis-educated and concluded that the latter was much worse.

Little has changed since Woodson's observations apart from the fact that it is not just the Negro who is subjected to years of mis-information. The masses, of whatever race, are subject to the same because the objective in modern education is still **'the mass-production of a work force'**.

Many of our schools and colleges operate like factories whose main function is to churn out workers. As a result, most people leave school with little or no self-employment skills and virtually no financial skills. This is tragic because without self-employment or financial skills, the masses are doomed to work for someone else who has them.

Mis-education is selective teaching in which the subjects that sustain the status quo are included whilst the subjects that enable authentic success are carefully and skillfully omitted.

It is my prayer that this book will begin to bridge the learning gap left by many years of mis-education and that the victims of mis-managed banks, greedy governments and unethical corporations will find hope in the knowledge that there is something they can do about it!

This book is therefore dedicated to the life and legacy of Carter G Woodson.

Wayne

www.thehomebusinessacademy.com

The Mis-Education of The Masses

What they didn't teach you at school

By Wayne Malcolm

Colleges are places where pebbles are polished and diamonds are dimmed.
Robert G. Ingersoll, Abraham Lincoln.

Introduction

No one saw it coming; neither banks nor governments, neither analysts nor economists, neither stock brokers or traders; or at least that's what they want us to believe! They want us to believe that the credit crunch, the global recession, the collapse of historic institutions, the unprecedented repossessions (foreclosure) of houses and escalating unemployment, just happened without warning and without notice.

If they couldn't see it coming, then how could we, the masses, who have had no financial education and really don't understand stock markets, money markets, inter-bank lending rates or even the true cost of credit. In fact we have all probably learned more about the world of money in the last 6 months than we did throughout our entire schooling, college or university years.

I wonder why money is not on the curriculum? It seems strange when you consider that so much of our adult life is spent in the pursuit of it and that so many of our problems as adults are linked to it. It strikes me as odd, that 95% of people in the developed world are financially illiterate and don't understand basics like:

- How do banks make money?
- How does credit scoring work?
- Who exactly is our country indebted to?
- Why were people on low incomes offered 100% mortgages?
- Who will pay for the bail out of banks and big corporations?

Financial illiteracy is no doubt the reason why most of us bought into the illusion of success created by the irresistible offer of easy credit. However, our ignorance clearly served the interests of a few, who profited from our limited vocabulary by veiling their deceptions in language that we were not trained to understand.

Consumer ignorance is not an accident. It is a carefully crafted and skilfully executed strategy to protect the interests of a few at the expense of the many. It really wouldn't help them if ordinary people could see through their scams and schemes designed to entice and enslave the unsuspecting. It wouldn't help their cause if the general public became financially literate. Worse yet it would cripple them if the public could read and understand their fine print or indeed if they discovered alternatives to credit.

Mis-education

Mis-education occurs when **'the promise of education is broken by the process of education.'** Education promises an equal opportunity for all and an increased capacity to achieve. However if the process itself omits or obscures the most important and critical subjects, then the whole experience is misleading and detrimental for the people who rely on it!

On the strategic level this is usually quite deliberate and calculated but on the operational and delivery level, teachers often have no idea that they are part of a plan to steer students towards one goal and away from another. This book attempts to show why the basic assumptions upon which our education system is built are no longer true. It also attempts to offer a strategy for those who realise that they have no option but to re-educate themselves for success!

Limited choices

When people make choices, they can only choose from the options that are available to them at the time. They typically choose the best of the options that they are aware of. Even if they make a bad or destructive choice, like joining a gang, they do so for reasons that seem good to them at the time or because it is the best of several options available to them.

The problem is that our perceived options are always limited by our level of knowledge and skill! For example, if you have no entrepreneurial knowledge, skills, tools or experience then your career choices are limited to a job or to government benefits or to crime. Starting your own business is not even considered, because it is simply not an option.

Mis-education occurs when realistic and sensible options are obscured by expectations that the student will go another way. In other words, if your education is designed to qualify and equip you for one option only, then it is easy to assume that it is the only option available. It may even become impossible to imagine another way.

When society expects it of you and parents want it for you and then school prepares you for it, you pretty much assume that it is the thing to do! Other options are simply off the radar. If you do later discover another way, you would literally have to re-educate yourself in order to comprehend it, let alone choose it!

Mis-educated

There is a big difference between being uneducated and being mis-educated. The uneducated person is basically uninformed while the mis-educated person has been misinformed and subsequently misled. The uneducated person is ignorant but knows it, while the mis-educated person is ignorant but doesn't know it.

Is it possible that the majority of people in the developed world were mis-educated and misled to embrace a formula and philosophy that only works for an elite few but that leaves the masses in misery? A formula that maintains the status quo and balance of power in favour of a few and at the expense of the many. A formula that is guaranteed to fail those who use it because it is based on a hidden agenda!

The game has changed

What if the game has changed but people are still being taught to play by the old rules and old strategies? What if they don't even know that the game has changed? This is exactly what lies at the root of our economic woes. We already live in a new economic era but the masses neither know it nor, more importantly, know what to do about it.

At the heart of our economic woes; rising inflation or deflation, deflating currencies, unprecedented job losses, bank failures, home repossessions, credit crunches and recessions, is the fact that **average people have been misled to rely on a formula that doesn't work!** Consequently they don't earn enough money, they are in debt, they are dependent on employers and governments and feel powerless to change their own circumstances for the better.

The masses receive little or no financial education, no leadership education, no business education and no success education. They are fundamentally educated for employment purposes and have no idea on how to achieve independence outside of the job market.

Even though the job market is shrinking so that more and more people are looking for fewer and fewer jobs, and in spite of the fact that no employer can guarantee you a job for life, we are still being educated for employment purposes, with a job being both the point and the prize of the whole process!

The process and the prize!

The result of this philosophy is mass disillusionment, suspicion and mis-trust of the whole system. Let me explain; many people fail in education because they don't think that the prize is worth the process. Remember, the prize in education is a job. If you do well you may even get a good job with plenty of prospects. However, the thought of long hours, low pay, a steep ladder and basically re-living their parents nightmare, doesn't particularly appeal to many youngsters.

Perhaps they are put off by the plight of those who do succeed in employment-based education? Those who succeed and achieve degree level often come out of the system in debt and are forced by desperation into jobs that are not even remotely related to the subjects that they studied at the highest level. I'm sure this all sounds bleak and that many will see this as an unfair or extreme position. However, what they cannot deny is the fact that few come through the system and into the dream that they were promised all along.

This book attempts to explore this phenomenon and to offer a way forward for people who want more for themselves and for their families.

If you want more then please read on.

Chapter 1

Educated For Employment

The chief wonder of education is that it does not ruin everybody concerned in it, teachers and taught.

> Henry Brooks Adams (1828-1918) U.S.
> historian and writer. The Education
> of Henry Adams.

The real prize in education is a good job. One with good prospects, plenty of perks and of course; great pay! The problem is that very few of these jobs actually exist (relatively speaking). This means that more and more people are looking for fewer and fewer jobs.

The other great prize is a vocational job that comes loaded with emotional rewards and real job satisfaction. Nursing, teaching, police work, emergency services, public services, social sector work and such like are all worthwhile pursuits. These may not offer the best pay scales but the emotional rewards often outweigh the pay problems. Anyone going into these professions to get rich may become disillusioned and should pay attention to the numbers of people in these sectors who have gone on strike over pay and conditions.

In reality, there are only a few good jobs and plenty of bad jobs. A bad job is one with little or no prospects, a toxic environment (both physically and socially), a boss who doesn't care about you, long hours, low pay, no security, few perks and boring tasks. Unfortunately most jobs sit in this category. People do these jobs for one reason and for one reason only; they need the money! If they won the lottery or inherited money, they would leave the job on the same day.

The new slave trade

People in this predicament are no better off than the African slaves were during the transatlantic slave trade. Racism was never the root of the slave trade; it was the result of it. The roots of the trade were all economic. The fact is that Europeans first sought to use their own indentured workers to grow sugar, tobacco and cotton in the Caribbean and the Americas, but they simply couldn't cope with the climate. They then found out that Africans lived and worked in similar climates and so decided to ship them from Africa to their work fields in the West.

They were effectively a cheap workforce for the empires of Britain, France, Spain and Portugal. Their job was to work the land and to generate income for their owners. They didn't work for nothing! They worked in exchange for a roof over their heads, a meal a day and some basic medical attention. They worked because they had no choice; the only other option was death.

The breaking house

Let me explain; when the slaves arrived in the West, they were first taken to a breaking house. Here the slaves were broken to believe that their future survival depended on their obedience to a slave master. They were taught to obey without question any command given by a slave owner. They were given new names and taught a new language made up of basic commands. They were also shown how they would be punished for any insurrection.

Once the slave was broken to believe that they had no future outside of a slave master, they were then brought to market. Rather like a job centre! Here, the slave masters would shop for new slaves to work in their fields. Of course, they would pick the best slaves for the best jobs and the worst for the worse jobs.

Were it not for the breaking house, the slave trade would have collapsed centuries before it did. The breaking house groomed, trained and prepared African princes for a life of slavery. It provided the essential training and disciplines needed to make a slave attractive to his future master. The best breaking houses produced the best workers, who then got the best slave masters and were rewarded with the best jobs.

Slave owners relied on breaking houses to churn out hard workers for their fields and projects. They were very concerned about getting a good deal because even though the labour was forced, it was still a costly exercise for the slave owner. After all, they had to buy the slave, keep the slave, train the slave and then work the slave to death. In exchange for this, the slave got to stay alive.

A striking parallel

Hopefully you can already see the striking parallels between the plight of the slaves and the plight of those who work hard at jobs they hate, for people they don't like and under conditions they cannot stand, just in order to make ends meet and to survive. Those who do it, do so because they were broken to believe that they have no choice. They were broken at school, college and university to believe that their future survival depended on them getting a job. They see no future for themselves outside of a job because they were given no training or tools for supporting themselves without one.

New chains

I know that the whips and chains have gone, but these have simply been replaced by more accept-able incentives, namely; debt and inflation. What forces people into a Just Over Broke job today is the rising cost of living and the carefully crafted debt trap. Debt is the new whip and inflation is the new chain that forces the masses into the misery of forced labour. I should add that in a recession, the rate of inflation and interest rates usually goes down drastically. But please don't be fooled by this; it occurs when fewer people are buying goods and services.

The real cost of living in these circumstances actu-ally goes up because money is harder to find. IT MAY EVEN BE IMPOSSIBLE TO FIND FOR PEOPLE WHO ARE JOB-DEPENDENT!

It is a mistake to make employment the sole point and prize in education. In fact it is misleading, when you consider the fact that the job market is shrinking so that fewer and fewer good jobs actually exist, and when you consider the fact that alternatives exist in abundance.

The alternative to employment is self-employment but this is only an option for those who have some entrepreneurial knowledge, skills and tools. Unfortunately these skills and tools are not readily available in formal education. Actually it is frowned on and deemed counterproductive because, they say, it spreads false hope? They wouldn't want students to believe that they could work for themselves and achieve independence outside of a job.

Yet, 95% of all those who achieve financial freedom, do so working for themselves and not for somebody else. When you meet a rich person, who is cash rich as opposed to credit rich, in almost all cases, you will find that they own their own businesses or that they work in fields where there are no limits on their capacity to earn.

Where do rich people come from?

If you meet a rich person, chances are they came from one or more of ten sources as follows:

1. **Inherited wealth** – Those who inherit wealth cannot be considered successful: just fortunate because they neither worked hard or smart for their wealth. They often don't know how to make money for themselves. In fact, in these circles, money is usually taken for granted and the means of making it is unclear. It is safe to say that most people reading this book did not inherit any substantial sums of money and will therefore have to take

the success route by learning how to make money for themselves.

2. **Corporate executive** – Energy, media, financial services, transportation, communications and more are all big business for those at the top of the earnings triangle. Executives and senior staff enjoy huge salaries, bonuses and perks. But all this comes at a price. First of all it takes years of working long hours, brown nosing, taking the blame and consistent performance before you'll even be considered for the top jobs.

   Getting into the industry is difficult enough let alone making it to the elite positions. In addition to this, barriers to entry like, race, gender and age are numerous and high. Corporate life is also merciless when it comes to performance. If the company underperforms; heads usually roll and departments get axed. At the time of writing this book, a major international bank announced that it was axing 50,000 jobs worldwide. This should confirm to one and all that corporate life is risky business.

3. **Real estate investing** – Even in the sub-prime mortgage crisis, savvy real estate investors are still making a killing by buying and selling repossessed (foreclosed) homes. They are also capitalising on the rise in rentals. Real estate investing is quite simple really; you buy real estate with someone else's money and then have some one else service the loan through rents. This idea has made

millions of people rich and yet this subject is not taught in any school, college or university. Perhaps it's not academic enough? Those who get involved in this business literally have to buy books, attend seminars and listen to audio programmes made by successful property investors in order to find out how to do it.

4. **Business ownership** – There are literally millions of small business opportunities in the world today. Some are ready made and come in the form of a franchise, whilst others can be started from scratch. However, success as a small business owner may escape you if you fail to learn from other people's mistakes. It may also escape you if you buy into the illusion of success that comes with easy credit and big overdrafts. Again, business ownership can make you rich and financially independent if you do it right!

5. **Commission based sales** – Please don't knock sales people! A sale is real business! It is the oldest business on earth and is the business upon which every other business is built. No sales, no business! Guess what; real business occurs at the point of a sale. Until money is exchanged for goods and services, there is no business in progress. Selling is an art, a science and a skill that can and must be developed by anyone who is serious about getting rich.

Effective selling is not about applying the pressure, neither is it about convincing people to buy things that they don't want or that they can't afford. It is about magnifying the value of a product or service until the price becomes minimal. More about this later!

6. **Stock investing** – In the current climate, it may be difficult to see how anyone is making money on the stock market. However make no mistake about it, people are still getting rich by buying and selling stocks. The reason is that they utilise numerous strategies for profiting from company stocks whether they rise or fall in value. They know what to buy, when to buy, how to buy and critically, when to sell. If you want to know how to do this, you'll have to attend the seminars of those who do it and then buy their books and audio products because this education is not readily available in schools, colleges or universities.

7. **Intellectual property** – Books, music, art and inventions all constitute intellectual property. Originators and creators can profit immensely from protecting, licensing and marketing their work; particularly in the internet age when individuals can go direct to market with their ideas and inventions. Although this strategy has made many people rich, it is still not presented as an option for the masses that are typically educated for employment purposes only.

Why aren't creativity, inventions and innovation on the curriculum? After all, It has a track record of lifting people out of poverty. People who live in impoverished neighbourhoods are often the most creative when it comes to music, art, inventions and poetry. They also learn quickly how to hustle. With the right training and tools many of them could transcend the expectations of teachers and eventually become rich. Instead of making this education available to the masses, it is typically discouraged by parents and teachers alike as an inferior and risky pursuit.

8. **Information marketing** - We live in the age of self-help in which more and more people want to know how they can do it themselves: whether it be making money, losing weight or enriching their relationships. We also live in a world of rapid change in which people are forced to keep abreast of current trends, new technology, new legislation and new opportunities. Those who can package and promote needed information can and have made a fortune. Information marketing has made many people rich and yet it is a virtually unknown phrase in formal education.

9. **Network marketing** – Network marketing has been around for about 50 years and yet it has lifted more people out of poverty than has any other business model. This is because it costs little or nothing to get started and has virtually no barriers to entry. It relies on word of mouth marketing and continues paying people even after they stop working. Some times known as multi-level marketing, this industry continues to evolve and upgrade its products, systems and compensation plans. It is undoubtedly the most available

option for people who don't want to go the employment route. Sadly very little is known about this reputable business model in employment-based education.

10. **Sports and entertainment** – These are undoubtedly the most visible and the most vocal of today's rich. Indeed, their visible fame and fortune continues to shape the aspirations of many young people who dream about becoming a footballer, an artist or a movie star. There also exists a plethora of magazines and TV shows that are dedicated to publishing their every move. However, what many do not realise is that only a tiny percentage of people in this game actually make a living from it and that only a small percentage of those actually go on to become rich.

The realities of celebrity life are also not clear to many who aspire to that status i.e. the hard work, the long hours, the level of competition, the barriers to entry, the multiple rejections and the loss of privacy. This route to riches has failed many more people than it has succeeded. If you have what it takes and your determination is unwavering then you can make it to the very top in sports and entertainment. But if you don't, or are not really serious, then please stop wasting your time and begin exploring the other options that have raised many regular people to riches.

Conclusion

Only seven of these ten have no barriers to entry. Only seven of these ten promise the possibility of time freedom along with financial freedom. Only seven of these ten are available to anyone who develops the skills necessary to run them and yet how many of these seven do you think are taught in schools? Absolutely none! So why is it that none of the strategies, subjects and skills that have proven to make people rich, are taught in school at any level? The answer is simple; these subjects do not produce employees; they produce employers! They do not inspire or encourage job seeking; they inspire independence, freedom and wealth creation.

Chapter 2

The Age of Job Insecurity

True education makes for inequality;
the inequality of individuality, the inequality
of success, the glorious inequality of talent,
of genius.

Felix E. Schelling (1858-1945)
American educator

No employer can guarantee you a job for life; they can't even guarantee that they will be in business this time next year. If you don't believe me, ask the 5000 employees of Lehman Brothers in London who were laid off with little notice when the company went into administration. Ask the 50,000 employees of the Citi-Banking Group whose jobs are being axed as I write. Ask the millions of people who are now looking for jobs as a result of the global economic crisis and credit crunch. All around us, historic institutions are closing down, banks have gone bankrupt and whole departments are being axed as companies merge and sell in a bid to stay afloat. This time last year, these events were unimaginable, but today they have finally laid to rest the illusion of job security.

A secure job?

The idea of a secure job was sold to the masses and promoted rigorously through education for years. However the old formula doesn't work. The old formula basically splits a persons life into three sections as follows:

1. First are the learning years from birth till about 25 years old. During this time we are expected to study hard and get the best qualifications so that we can get a secure job with plenty of pay and perks.

2. Then comes the earning years when we are expected to get a secure job, work our way up the ladder and hold the job down for life.

3. Finally comes the yearning years when we realise that the whole formula doesn't work and we wish that we knew then, what we know now. Unfortunately for the masses, this epiphany does not occur until they are freezing cold in a council (government) apartment and can't afford to put on the heating.

Although this formula has failed most people who tried it, many parents are still content to pass it on to their children. Many teachers are happy to teach it to their pupils and the vast majority of people in society still think that it is the only way to go.

At this point, I should make something abundantly clear; I think that teachers are amongst the most noble, honourable and valuable people in our society. I think they are grossly under paid and grossly over worked. I think they are amazing. My criticism is not of teachers or professors. After all they are employed to teach curriculums that they didn't write and over which they have little or no control. Their job is to deliver the lessons and to hit the targets that they are given. They have very little room to manoeuvre and must stick to the programme or lose their own job.

My problem is with the system that still insists on educating people for employment purposes only and that omits the subjects that are proven to produce wealth. I am disturbed at the thought that the masses are being trained exclusively for a job when few good jobs actually exist and the age of job insecurity is clearly upon us. I am further concerned that the masses are being mis-guided by an educational philosophy that is inadequate, antiquated, irrelevant and misleading.

An alternative exists!

The good news is that an alternative formula exists. This formula says that **what you learn determines what you earn!** If you learn real estate investing, then you can earn real-estate investing money. If you learn marketing and sales, then you can earn marketing and sales money. If you learn information marketing, then you can earn the information marketers money. If you learn network marketing then you can earn network-marketing money. However if all your learning was designed to qualify you for a job, then you will have limited yourself to earning job-money.

The difference between job money and the other forms of money described in this book is the difference between thousands and millions. Job money is usually limited to less than £30,000.00 a year. The exceptions to this rule, only apply to 10% of the working population in Britain who earn in excess of £35,000 per year. Independent business money on the other hand is typically limitless and can produce millions for people who start early and work smart. I know network marketers who earn £30,000.00 per month. They all failed at school and lived in relative poverty before taking up network marketing. They also achieved this level of income within three years of starting the business.

I also know information marketers and Internet marketers who earn in excess of £30,000.00 per month. They went into the business because there are no academic, age, gender, class or racial barriers to entry and were then able to achieve personal fortunes within 3 years.

The philosophy of dependence

The masses are still being taught a philosophy of dependence, even though we clearly live in the age of independence. The philosophy of dependence basically says; **'my future lies in the hands of an employer or the government.'** For example, when the elite students leave university, they immediately begin competing for jobs. They do this religiously as though this is the only thing they can do. After all, that is why they studied so hard and achieved a degree; so they can compete for the best jobs. Likewise when people, not so bright, leave school with less than the best grades, they are encouraged to compete for lower paying jobs. The only alternative is to claim benefits from the government.

Someone obviously taught them that the only way to get money is from an employer or from the government. If this is not dependence, then what is? The philosophy of dependence, dis-empowers people by taking control out of their own hands and putting it into the hands of the government and industry. It renders them helpless and powerless when it comes to generating income.

On the other hand, the philosophy of independence is the way of the entrepreneur. This philosophy says, **'with the right training and tools, I can create multiple income streams as a self-employed entrepreneur.'** This philosophy enables people to both see and to seize opportunities to make money. It steers their thinking away from the box and induces a state of creativity. It awakens the power of ideas, innovation, initiative and invention. It fosters self-determination, self-reliance and self-control. It is the driving force behind self-education, which is the driving force behind self-empowerment.

The entrepreneurial mind

Just because an employer won't give you a job, doesn't mean that you have to join the queue for government benefits. Thankfully, there is an alternative, namely; to start your own business ventures as an independent entrepreneur. This may sound too good to be true for people who were mis-educated and believe that entrepreneurs are academics from a wealthy background. The facts are that most entrepreneurs:

• Didn't do well at school,
• Did not inherit wealth

- Can remember being poor
- Started out their ventures with little or nothing
- Were cash-poor but ideas and discipline-rich when they went into business.

I know that business studies are taught at school, college and university, however the objective of the education is never business ownership. The objective is always a job! Youngsters who take up business studies are usually seeking to enter the job market at a higher level. It is hoped that the best students will be earmarked for a management role within a company but not that they will use their skills to go into business for themselves. Likewise, when they are taught trades like mechanics and plumbing, it is so that they can get a job working for a mechanic or a plumber. The self-employment options are seldom discussed and in some cases completely avoided.

Omitting the critical subject

This approach amounts to an act of gross mis-education because it has produced gross ignorance about the **one subject that could make people rich, namely; entrepreneurship and business ownership!** The gross ignorance of the masses when it comes to business is evidenced by the fear, suspicion and avoidance of business people and opportunities to create lasting wealth. So lets set the record straight:

Entrepreneurs drive the world forward: Wherever you are sitting right now and whatever you can see, was made possible by the entrepreneurial mind. Are you sitting in an armchair? Is there a TV in the room?

Is it a house or an apartment? Perhaps you're on a plane? All of these luxuries represent progress for the human family and each of them were invented, marketed and sold by entrepreneurs.

What do the clothes on your back have in common with the car you drive and the food you eat? They were all produced, packaged, priced and promoted by entrepreneurs. Indeed, the job market itself owes its existence to the entrepreneurial mind. A work force is simply the body of an entrepreneurial head because it gives hands and feet to an entrepreneurial idea. Without business owners, there would be no jobs. Without entrepreneurs there would be no goods in the stores and no stores for your goods.

Entrepreneurs create the connections and build the bridges that unite the demand side of the market with the supply side. They are the critical component and king pin of growing economies. They are also the missing link in failing or shrinking economies.

The history of recession shows a consistent pattern in the way that countries bounce back from an economic break down. The pattern is as follows; **'when people can't get jobs and the government wont help, they start looking inwards for ideas and outwards for opportunities to make their own money.'** In other words, recession tends to wake up the entrepreneur within us by forcing us to find another way to survive. So that while traditional markets shrink, new markets begin to emerge. While old systems fall, they make way for new once to rise. While old assumptions fail, new philosophies appear.

This pattern is well documented and even studied at university level. In fact if you listen closely to the commentators and experts today, they are already suggesting that we must now embrace a new way of thinking, a new way of living and a new way of doing business. They are now openly saying that entrepreneurship is the way out of this recession.

The illusion of success

The bubble has well and truly burst. I am referring to the illusion of success created by credit in all its forms. Buy now and pay later, store cards, credit cards, loans, finance deals and overdrafts. The global economic crisis that has put banks out of business and huge companies into administration all begun with the sub-prime mortgage crisis. These were mortgages given to people who were considered a high risk. Bankers found a way to make a quick profit from these doggy deals by packaging them together with good deals and then selling the whole bundle on to other banks.

For the masses, it was the irresistible offer for people who had unpredictable incomes, poor credit ratings and a history of debt. It meant that they could now borrow the money to buy homes and cars. However what they really bought with borrowed money was the illusion of success.

The result was that people lived in homes they didn't own, drove cars they didn't own, sat for dinner at tables they didn't own, relaxed on a couch they didn't own, watched a TV they didn't own and then got a drink from a fridge they didn't own before retiring for the night in a bed they didn't own. Even though they had borrowed 95% and in some cases 100% of the money for these purchases, they still embraced the illusion that they owned these things. When they couldn't keep up with the payments, they were then devastated by the attitude of the banks that now re-possessed their home and its contents.

Although this bubble has now burst and people are beginning to realise that easy credit only buys an illusion, they still don't realise that **this is the only success available to most employees.** A job can make you credit rich but not cash rich. Like I've said before, the point and the prize in education is a good job. However the point and the prize in a good job is easy credit. Just as good qualifications only serve to qualify you for a good job; a good job only serves to qualify you for good credit and all good credit can purchase for you is the illusion of success.

You cannot purchase a beautiful leather sofa with one cash payment from your monthly earnings. There are a few who can, but they are the top 5% of the highest earners. However with a good job, you can qualify for a store card or a credit card or a financing deal. Hey presto, the beautiful leather sofa arrives, followed shortly by a statement.

But what if you lost your job? It's not a bad question given the current climate. If you lost your job, you would eventually lose your home and its contents because they are not really yours until you pay back the loan company that borrowed you the money to purchase them in the first place. Make no mistake about it; the loan company does not care about you, your children or your mother. They care about getting their money back with interest.

The good news is that with the right training and the best tools you can generate multiple incomes and become cash rich by working for yourself. The great news is that it is easier to do this in today's world than it has ever been in the history of the world. Remember this; a good job can at most make you credit rich, but a great business system can make you cash rich!

Read on to find out how.

Chapter 3

The New Economic Era

Education ... has produced a vast population able to read but unable to distinguish what is worth reading.

G. M. Trevelyan (1876-1962)
British historian

We are already living in a new economic era in which the new game can only be played and won by the people who know the new rules. Sadly, the masses are still being mis-educated into playing the old game by the old rules. Hopefully by now, you'll agree with me that the old game doesn't work even for those who win it because at best it can only make you credit rich, which in turn will only buy you **the illusion of success.**

This is not just true of individuals; it is also true of companies that are still playing the old game by the old rules. The tradition business model is based on credit. Here is how it works; you develop a business plan complete with projections and forecasts and then you take it to the bank and ask them to finance the business until it breaks even, or to provide a cash safety net should it fall into difficulties. In exchange for this, the bank will usually ask for some security in the form of a charge over the business and over your personal assets.

This is the business model employed by every business that is currently in crisis. It is the business model taught by business schools and it is considered by many to be the only way to set up a sustainable business. Both big and small businesses operate this way. This is why airlines, car manufacturers and even banks have gone into administration. It is because their banks and financiers were no longer convinced that they would get a return on their investments and therefore decided to pull the plug.

Pulling the plug

The same phenomenon occurs in the public sector when the government finances projects. If the government agency pulls the plug, the business goes under because it was never making enough money to support itself in the first place. It was never self-sustaining or commercially viable. It was simply qualified for credit but was never a credible market force.

The real problem with this business model is the many barriers to entry that make it virtually impossible for ordinary people to go into business. To qualify for a business loan, a person would have to produce an impeccable credit history, the relevant qualifications, security for the loan and be willing to surrender control of the business to the lender. Besides that, they also need to have the right age, the right height, the right gender, the right shape, the right facial features, the right shade, the best references and the right vocabulary before the banks will even take them seriously.

These criterions excluded the masses from the business arena. However today there are a growing number of business opportunities that come with none of these barriers to entry. In fact, the emerging market for independent entrepreneurs is colour blind, age blind and gender blind. It is also totally blind to your credit history.

It doesn't care if you are short, fat, thin, ugly or pretty because it only uses banks to deposit money but never to borrow it. Academic qualifications are helpful but not essential in this field. *So if you failed at school, don't worry because even though you will be excluded from the best job offers and from business loans, you won't be excluded from the arena of success.*

The age of the independent!

We have come through the industrial age and are now living in the age of the independent, in which the number one employer is going to be SELF! The industrial revolution of the late 1800's ushered us into the industrial age of mass employment by industry sectors. During this period, the driving force behind the economy of the developed world was manufacturing, mass production, factories and machinery.

The mis-education of the masses is, in fact, a by-product of the industrial age. The focus on employment-based education came out of the era of job abundance from factory floors in which people were basically trained to do jobs. This was the opportunity and the prize that education promised and this was the goal for most people.

However by the 1960's three factors began to signal the end of the industrial age, namely; the service industry, globalisation and technology. The service age saw the rise of service-based industries like financial services. This meant that people could now choose between working on products in a factory and delivering services to people directly.

When this revolution occurred, most people found themselves ill-equipped to capitalise on the new opportunities. All of a sudden, service based industries had to develop training programmes designed to deliver people skills to their work forces because factory skills and mind-sets could not support a service based industry.

NB: It is important to note that the emergence of a new economic era does not mean the disappearance of the old, it simply constitutes a replacement of the old as the driving force behind the economy. It also means that those who cleave to the old, get left behind by those who capitalise on the new.

From the service age, we moved into the information age in which the highest paid workers used their minds to work on projects whilst the lowest paid workers still used their hands to work on products. Information became the new land, the new gold and the new oil. It is the age of mind power that replaced the age of manpower. Whole industries emerged trading in knowledge, information, technology and skills. Out of this came the Internet as an information-sharing tool and from that point on, a super economic era was born!

Opportunity for independents

I call it the age of independence. It is the age of opportunity for independent entrepreneurs who understand the possibilities that globalisation and technology have created for individuals. Globalisation means the erosion of trade barriers. It means that individuals in England can buy from companies in China and individuals in Poland can buy from companies in Russia without the typical trade barriers that characterised the industrial age. This is why call centres in India now service customers in England and America.

Globalisation has created fierce competition for companies that must now compete with foreign suppliers for local business. For example, when I produced my first musical album, I had the option of printing and pressing my CD's in the UK or in Eastern Europe. The company in England charged £1.50 per unit to press and print my CD's. However the company in Eastern Europe charged 37p per unit for the same quality and quantity. Of course I used the Eastern European company and the UK Company lost out on my business. For the first time in history I can choose to shop in China, Poland or Japan for my goods and services. I can even choose to have this book printed in America, China or Africa and am no longer limited to a UK printer.

The miracle is that I can do all of this from my living room because of the Internet. When fused with technology, in the form of high-speed communications; globalisation has created more choice for consumers and therefore new opportunities for independent entrepreneurs.

Internet magic

The magic of the Internet is that it allows individuals to market products and services to a worldwide audience, without the consent or support of the industry. The ability to go direct to market used to be the privilege of big industries, but thanks to technology, that has changed. Now individuals can achieve by themselves what was once only possible for a big company.

For example, years ago, if you wanted to become a singer, you had to go, cap in hand to the music industry. Only a major record label had the power to make you a star because they alone owned the means of producing, marketing and distributing music. Today, thanks to technology, an artist can write, produce and distribute their own music to a global audience from the comforts of their own home using software and the Internet.

- They can produce their own music using software like Logics, Fruity Loops or Pro Tools
- They can produce their own music videos using software like Final Cut Pro,
- They can air their own music video's on You Tube, (which has hundreds of millions of users worldwide).

- They can promote their music to millions through social networking sites like MySpace and other digital platforms
- They can sell their own music from their own website or from an established digital platform like itunes.
- They no longer have to press CD's but if they want to they can use print on demand services like Lulu.com

As a result of these new possibilities we have seen the rise of independent record labels, radio stations, TV channels, publishers, agencies, brokers, retailers, marketers and more. Further to this, because established companies rely on sales, they are usually willing to pay commissions and rewards to anyone who can bring the business their way. **This means that individuals can now market and sell virtually any thing to anyone, anywhere and get paid for it.** Even if they are not qualified to sell a particular service (i.e. financial services), they can still get paid for referrals that lead to a sale.

Business from your bedroom

Think about it, you can now go into business from your bedroom or from your living room or on holiday or from anywhere in the world that you can get online. You don't even have to have a product of your own. You can become an affiliate agent of an existing company and get paid for promoting their products to your own network. If you do have your own prod-uct, you can go direct to market in any country that is Internet ready.

Of course this opportunity is only available to people who have the right training and the best tools. Unfortunately the training and tools necessary to capitalise on this emerging market is not available in employment-based education. It is currently only available from gurus and experts who are currently making a fortune from direct marketing strategies. These people understand the real business behind real business and have decided to concentrate their efforts there.

The real business behind real business

Real business occurs at the point of a sale. As simple as this concept seems, it is often forgotten by traditional companies that are credit rich. These companies tend to under invest in sales and to over invest in overheads and processes. However the truth is that you are not in business until money is exchanged for your goods and services. The fact that you produce, manufacture, invent or create does not put you in business. You are only running a successful business if your revenue from sales exceeds the cost of running the company. It's simple, but profound. No sales, no business!

However, there is a business that under girds the real business of sales. I call it the real business behind real business. You guessed it, its marketing! Marketing is not simply one of many business functions, neither is it a department in the company; it is the business! A leading cause of failure in business is the failure to understand what business you are actually in. Whatever business you think you are in, the real business is marketing. Authors are really in the book marketing business. Singers are really in the music marketing business. Restaurant owners are really in the experience-marketing business. Travel agents also are in the experience marketing business and on and on.

If an author fails to understand this fact, they may become a best **writing** author, but they will never become a best **selling** author. Likewise if a singer fails to understand the real business of marketing music, they may make the best songs but they will not make it in the charts. If a restaurant owner thinks that they are in the food business, they will concentrate on serving the best meals but will never be able to compete with those who are in the business of marketing a food-based experience.

Why marketing is the core skill

Let me explain why marketing is the core business at the root of the real business of exchanging money for goods and services. I should start by saying that marketing for traditional companies and even for some business schools amounts to little more than advertising and promotions. However, authentic marketing is much more profound than advertising and promotions. Authentic marketing is based on the fundamental forces of supply and demand.

The basis of all business is the law of supply and demand. This law basically says; if you can supply what people demand, they will pay you for it. This means that there are two sides to an economy, namely the demand side which constitutes peo-ple or organisations with needs and the supply side which is represented by people and organisations that have goods and services for sale.

Although marketing involves sales, promotion and publicity stunts; it is not fundamentally any of these for the following reasons:

- Sales, advertising and promotions are all designed to serve and support the supply side of the market.
- Authentic marketing on the other hand is designed to serve and support the demand side of the market.

This is what differentiates pure marketing from promotion, advertising and sales. Authentic marketers will never position themselves on the supply side of the market, they will always position themselves on the demand side. This means that they refuse to start their business with a product or service, instead they start with an established need. They typically start by listening to consumers, observing trends and identifying opportunities to satisfy customers. They won't even introduce a product or service that is not in demand because their allegiance does not lie with any product or brand; instead it lies with people and their needs.

Expert marketing

To become an expert marketer, you must break any addictions that you have to your product and instead become addicted to meeting your customer's needs. You must become an asset to customers by always acting in their interests. If your loyalty lies with suppliers, you would be better off as a sales person because an authentic marketer is only loyal to customers.

Those who are making a fortune in the emerging market for independent entrepreneurs, created by globalisation and technology, are doing so by concentrating on the core skill of marketing. Whatever the product they sell, their true skill and core capacity is marketing goods, experiences, services and hope to people who are already looking for these things. In this respect marketing is the same as building a bridge between the demand side of the market and the supply side. The bridge starts with customer demands for new, better, cheaper or friendlier services or goods and then ends up with a supplier who is willing to give real value for money.

Here is what marketers do:

Detect the demand – this comes by listening to consumers, analysing trends and finding the gaps. Typically they fish for the pain, the pressure and the problems facing consumers and businesses. They also fish for aspirations and ambition.

Source a supply – this means finding solutions for consumers and businesses that offer real value for money. It means finding what enough people are already looking for.

Create the connection – this comes in the form of what is called the marketing mix of offering the right product, at the right price, in the right packaging, with the right promotion and in the best position.

If you can develop the core skill of marketing, the world will become your oyster because you can use it to make a fortune serving the interests, aspirations and concerns of multiple niche markets. The great news is that you can now do all of this from your home, from abroad or from anywhere in the world.

Authentic sales

Marketers are not the same as sales people. The main difference is that sales people are usually promoters and persuaders while marketers are typically educators and informers. An authentic marketer is in the business of educating consumers about products and services that are already in high demand. In this respect they support consumer interests, aspirations and concerns. If there is no demand, marketers are not interested in the supply. Sales people, on the other hand, are often limited by the product they are commissioned to sell. They typically end up convincing people to buy something that they really don't want.

The persuasive tactics of persuasive sales people are based on a fundamental misunderstanding of what authentic selling really involves. It is also based on a misunderstanding of the psychology of motivation. People are not moved to act by gloss and gimmicks; they are moved to the point of sale by a **split-second cost/value analysis.** Authentic sales people know how to magnify the value of a product or service to the end user because they know that when the value is maximised the price is automatically minimised.

For example, if I offer you a coat for £50.00, you may analyse it to see if it fits and if it is worth £50.00 to you. £50.00 may seem like too much money to spend on a coat that you're not sure about. However if I offer you my car for £50.00, the same money looks like peanuts compared to what you get in exchange for it.

The golden rule then is that the cost is only an issue when the value is too small. That is why authentic marketers become expert educators who know how to amplify and magnify the value of products and services to the end user. This process only begins once the marketer is clear about the outcomes or results that the buyers are really looking for.

Remember this: people do not really buy products and services; they buy outcomes and results. Marketers know this but sales people often don't.

Niche markets:

The biggest opportunity for independent entrepreneurs is the use of technology to market goods and services to a global audience. It is a low cost opportunity with no barriers to entry and if done right can deliver money freedom, time freedom, freedom of mobility and freedom of expression.

Nowhere is this opportunity more evident than in niche markets. A niche market is effectively a special interest group. These could be pet owners, sports enthusiasts, business opportunity seekers, health addicts, romantics, parents or lovers of hip-hop. Most high street retailers do not cater for special interest groups and that is why they have to look beyond the high street for the products and services that meet their unique set of needs.

There are potentially millions of niche markets in the world. Each niche provides an opportunity for independent marketers to source solutions and to create connections between the demanders and the suppliers.

For example, I have a friend who specialises in brand-less technology. The technology is manufactured in China and is made to order. This company allows people to put their own brands and logos on various gadgets like MP4 players, cameras and mobile phones, whilst providing the technical support and guarantees through their partners worldwide. My friend doesn't buy the technology; he simply markets the technology to entrepreneurs who wish to create their own brand of technology. He also markets these novelties to associations and networks that wish to add them to their product catalogue. His office is his house and his primary tool is his computer.

I have another friend who specialises in hip-hop phones. These phones come in gold plate, solid gold, and even platinum. They are typically diamond encrusted and come with a variety of hip-hop ring tones. My friend doesn't buy these phones but he does market them to artists within the hip-hop community.

Again he works from home with his computer.

Most of my friends simply sell information online to niche markets. These typically come in the form of e-books, audio programmes and how-to guides. My friends are not always the authors of these programmes but they do have the rights to sell them. The information is extremely valuable to niche markets who simply can't get the information in a book-store or even from an online bookstore. Information based products typically sell from anywhere between £20 and £2,000.00. This means that if you marketed a £20.00 information-based product to a niche market that couldn't get the information from regular stores, you would only need 5000 sales in order to make £100,000. It also means that if the product costs £200.00, you would only need 5000 sales worldwide in order to turn over your first million.

When it comes to niche marketing; size really does matter! The basic rule is this: the smaller, the better! In other words the more special the interest, the more willing they will be to pay above-average prices for the information, products or services. If you can demonstrate an appreciation of their issues, aspirations and concerns, they will come to see you as a giver to, 'and not a taker from' their community.

When you understand this, it is easy to see how online marketers generate multiple incomes from multiple web sites that are positioned within niche markets around the world. It should also explain why marketing is the core business of these entrepreneurs. They know that once the skills are developed they can use them to accelerate any business opportunity that comes their way.

www.thehomebusinessacademy.com

Chapter 4

Mis-Information

We are shut up in schools and college recitation rooms for ten or fifteen years, and come out at last with a bellyful of words and do not know a thing.

Ralph Waldo Emerson (1803-82)
U.S. essayist and poet.

Mis-education is the process of misinforming people about the options and choices available to them in the modern world. Here are eight of the most common forms of misinformation promoted through mis-education:

1. Majoring in minors

Much of the information deemed important in education has no relationship with normal life or with a person's earning potential. Students are often forced to remember facts that they will never need to remember throughout the course of their working life. What's worse is that they are then judged and accessed by their ability to remember and articulate these facts.

Indeed, the reason why it is becoming increasingly difficult for teachers to keep the attention of youngsters in urban and deprived areas, is the complete irrelevance of the subjects being taught. Why would you teach people struggling with deprivation about the antics of Henry VIII or about a classic piece of english literature? More importantly, why should their level of intelligence be judged by their ability to remember and articulate these facts?

I'm not suggesting that these facts are not important; just that they are minor compared with the major issues facing such people. For example, most people receive no financial education at school even though most of their adult life will revolve around money. Likewise most people receive no leadership or entrepreneurial training during their formal education, even though self-employment is a viable and potentially lucrative alternative to job-dependency. Social skills training is likewise not deemed a priority even though it is commonly known that opportunities in life are most available to the people who have high levels of social skills.

Please don't get me wrong, I am all for formal education, I just believe that much of the curriculum is outdated and irrelevant. I am also suspicious of a curriculum that does nothing to prepare people for success in life. After all, the purpose of education is to prepare dependent youngsters for independence as an adult. The end result of spending our tender years majoring in minors is that we end up spending our working years minor-ing in majors.

World-class martial artists, gymnasts, boxers and business people all acquired an interest in their field during their tender years. Thankfully they had smart adults in their life who ensured that these interests were not pushed aside in favour of less important subjects but instead nurtured and supported them until they became fruitful.

The mis-educated masses were taught how to read but not what to read. They were taught mathematics, but not how to apply this to a domestic budget or to a business plan.

2. Job dependency

The credit crunch is biting everybody, but it is absolutely killing job-dependent people whose only hope of earning money and paying their bills lies in the hands of an employer. These masses were mis-educated by a system that made employment both the point and the prize in education. They were sold the old formula as follows: 'study hard so you can get good qualifications, so you can compete for the best jobs.' So that's what they did. They studied hard at school, college and university so that they could land a good job. In the process, of course, they became job-dependent.

Job–dependency means; having no skills for generating income outside of a job. The job dependent person has one goal, one hope and one strategy for living, namely landing a good job. The problem with this philosophy is that the job market is shrinking, shaking and sinking at the prospect of a global recession. This means millions of job losses worldwide and it also means more people looking for fewer jobs.

The biggest casualties of the credit crunch and global recession are the job-dependants who must now join the queue and wait in line for another job or look to the government for support, interventions and benefits.

Where do you think so many job-dependants came from? They came right out of our educational system. Year after year, thousands of them flood the markets in search of jobs. What else can they do? They have spent years in training for this very thing. Even if they took business studies at school, the objective was never to go into business but rather to go into somebody else's business at a slightly higher entry level.

Job dependency is a sad condition and its true tragedy is going to become ever more visible in difficult times. It would not surprise this author if we entered a season of civil unrest and dis-obedience as a result of the fact that we created a job dependent-society and then took away the jobs.

Of course the answer to job-dependency is job independence however this is only an option for people who have re-educated themselves in the art and science of self-generated income.

3. Solo income

Not only were the masses mis-educated into a state of job-dependency, they were also mis-educated to rely on a solo income. The idea of one income stream is foreign to rich people but all too common for poor people. So let's make this clear; **rich people enjoy multiple income streams whilst poor people rely on a solo income.**

The reason why the solo income idea is so popular is that most people get their income from a job in which they exchange time for money; usually no less than 8 hours a day and increasingly as much as 10 and 12 hours a day. This schedule leaves little time left for anything else when they are finished.

The idea of trading time for money is tragic because your time is infinitely more valuable than money. If you run out of money, you can always get some more but if you run out of time, then its all over. In fact there is no difference between your time and your life. If you swap the word time for life, then certain popular phrases would take on new meaning like; that was a waste of time or this is time-consuming or there is not enough time in the day. You would quickly realise that it is your life being wasted and consumed or that there isn't enough life in your day.

Multiple incomes are only possible for people who know how to **'dig a well.'** Digging a well is hard, however once the work is done, it keeps giving you water for life. This is called passive or low-maintenance income. It does require a great deal of initial work, but once the work is done, it just keeps making money for you while you sleep.

For example, once this book is published, it will become a source of passive income for me because long after I have stopped writing this book, it will continue to sell. The same is true of any automated business system. An automated business system is one that generates income with little or no maintenance because the systems are fully automated.

This is the core difference between entrepreneurs and business people. Many business people are not entrepreneurs; they simply run a business. The entrepreneur is not interested in running a business at all; they are interested in owning a profit-making business system. They will work hard to build a business system that will make money for them after they stop working on it; a business that will continue to pay them while they are playing golf or yachting in the Caribbean. Once the system is built, they move on and build another, then another, then another.

Passive income is only an option for people who know how to create it. This unfortunately excludes the masses who were mis-educated to rely on a solo-income from their one good job. True independence is the privilege of those who can dig wells. Initially, this may have to be done in your spare time, but when your income from your wells overtakes your income from your job, you can move into the lucrative business of generating multiple streams of passive income.

The great news is that the new economic era has created more opportunity for individuals to create passive incomes from the comforts of their own home.

4. Scarcity

Another piece of mis-information that has been fed to the masses is the doctrine of scarcity. This doctrine says that there is not enough to go around, everybody can't be rich and that we should be grateful and content with what little we have. The truth is that we live in an abundant world with more than enough for everyone to have more than enough. Actually, there is enough wealth on planet earth for every one of its 6 billion people to become a millionaire several times over.

This means that there is no shortage of money, there is no shortage of opportunity and there is no shortage of resources for people who know how to get at it. For example, It would only cost £200b to settle the entire debt of the entire continent of Africa. Yet for years this has seemed like an impossible task. There simply wasn't enough money to make this happen. Yet in recent months we have seen both Britain and America commit twice this amount to prop up failing banks. Where did that money come from? It is enough money to build hundreds of schools, hospitals, better transportation, better pay and dare I say it, new jobs. Yet before the credit crisis, this money was simply not available. It didn't exist!

Scarcity is an illusion that serves the interests of a few at the expense of the many who buy into it. Disparity on the other hand is a fact. The growing gap between the income of the rich and the income of the poor is proof of the fact that one group has been groomed for business ownership while the other has been mis-educated to become job-dependents on solo incomes.

If you consider the amount of food that is thrown away by restaurants each night in any developed city, you will realise that poverty and hunger, anywhere in the world, are totally man-made and completely un-necessary.

This is important because it explains why people opt for the insecurity of job dependency and a solo income; it is their belief in the doctrine of scarcity. They figure that there probably are not any good business opportunities left, or that the competition in business is too high or that there are not enough people who can afford to spend on their special interests.

5. Filthy rich

Another bi-product of misinformation is the belief that there is something inherently wrong with being rich. Many people come through an employment-based education as incurable **richer-phobics.** A richer-phobic is someone who mistrusts and in some cases despises the rich. They see them as the cause of all problems social, economical and political. They are seen as the reason for famine, war and global poverty. This is ultimately what is meant by popular phrases like; filthy rich!

Again, this is a spill over from previous economic eras, when the ruling classes amassed their riches through oppressing and exploiting the poor. However the majority of today's self-made millionaires achieved their success through initiative, ingenuity and intelligence. Their riches are a reflection of the fact that they have managed to supply what the market demands. Their money is a mirror, reflecting the value that they have added to thousands and millions of lives.

In today's world, the way to wealth is to enrich others. If you want to become rich you will have to sell goods, services or information to people who want to buy them. Unfortunately, those who were mis-educated to become job-dependent still see the rich as suspicious characters who deserve to be taxed to the max and in some cases even robbed. Such beliefs act as real barriers to success because they are based on a fundamental misunderstanding of how money is generated. Put simply; it is exchanged for goods, services and information that are in demand.

In addition to this, there is the failure to see that this very exchange is the platform of progress for nations, and indeed the world. It is entrepreneurs in both the private and the public sector that are responsible for transportation, energy, buildings, furniture, technology, science, medicine and more. The time and energy invested in the creation and production of these things later gets compensated when these goods are exchanged for money.

The good news is that in between the concept and the customer there are often employees who then get the benefit of a monthly income which means more spending, more demand, more supply and on and on. In this respect, it is the business person who creates jobs, which in turn pays for public services through income tax and which creates more jobs by enabling people to buy.

I can tell that some of you at this point are confused; I thought he was against jobs? No I'm not, I am simply pro-choice and I think that a decent education should equip people to choose. Richer-phobia is based on ignorance of what it takes to become rich and of how much better the world would be if more people had more money!

6. Retirement:

The old formula that has failed so many people says that you should save during your working life so that you can retire at 65yrs and then rely on those savings to support you till you die. Those who don't earn enough to save for retirement are expected to contribute to a government fund that promises to provide them a pension during retirement.

The mis-educated masses tend to follow this formula without question because they have never been introduced to another possibility. Indeed no other options exist within the job sector. However outside of the limitations of a job, there exists a plethora of options.

But before we explore these options lets first look at the mis-information upon which the old formula is based. The old formula suggests that retirement should be the golden years of reward in which we reap the benefits of all the hard work and savings made during your working years. The theory is that if you work hard enough and save enough, then you can retire on a pension that delivers a more luxurious life than the one you are use to. It is expected that people should be prudent and frugal while they work, so that they can be liberal and splash out in later life.

First of all, how do you know that you will retire at age 65? How do you know that you will even live that long or that your health will permit you to enjoy your pension? How can the government guarantee that it will take care of you? The whole formula is a gamble both on the part of the pensioner and on the part of the government who are continuously raising the age of retirement in an attempt to reduce the years of responsibility.

All of these ideas constitute the rolling of the dice, or a gamble that it will all work out in the end. However, the vast majority of people following this formula would not do it again if they had another life to live. This is particularly true of those who have given the most to their country as soldiers, nurses, police officers, teachers and more.

There is of course another formula, however it is only available to those people who have re-educated themselves to achieve job independence. Job independence is the freedom to work for yourself on the creation of passive and residual incomes. It is the business of creating wealth, which is not the same as making money. The difference is the difference between the water and the well. The water represents money, while the well represents wealth. The water comes from the well because the well is its source. In this respect, job-independence means owning your own money source.

The masses were mis-educated to pursue water, while the new rich were re-educated to dig wells. The down side of well digging is that while you are digging, you may become very thirsty and need to buy water from someone who already has a well. But once your well is dug and water is struck, you have created for yourself a life-long income.

There are only a few business opportunities that offer a residual income. Network marketing is one of them. Many network-marketing companies are reviewing their compensation plan to include lucrative residual incomes for those who successfully build a high performing team. Likewise many affiliate marketing programmes now include a residual income package for those who significantly increase their sales. Residual income means doing the work once and then getting paid for it every month for life. This is by no means easy to achieve but many have done it within one year of starting out in network marketing.

Passive income is likewise an income that kicks in after the work is done. This form of income is usually generated through the sale of intellectual property. Information, books, study guides, songs, poetry, art, inventions or photography can produce regular royalties if licensed and marketed well.

Passive income is the objective in business. At least for entrepreneurs who go into business with a clear sense of objective. These people, who get to retire several times throughout their working life, are not as interested in running a business as they are in owning one. Owning a business is like owning a well, because the business is fundamentally a money source. They know that they will have to run it for a while, but that when the system is fully automated they can then employ someone to take on their roll. At that point they can sell it, franchise it or float it on the stock exchange because they no longer need to work in it in order to make it work. This is known in business as an exit route or strategy. It is only possible for entrepreneurs who have literally created an automated money machine.

The alternative to the old retirement formula is to create passive incomes that allow you to take several mini-retirements throughout your strong years, whilst building an asset base for your weaker years.

7. Government benefits

Of course an option for job-dependents who lose their job is government benefits. However what is not always realised is that government benefits are carefully calculated to the penny so that claimers receive just enough to survive if they are frugal and shop in the cheapest stores. In short, government benefits are meant to be uncomfortable and unbearable so that people move into jobs as quickly as possible.

Just in case you still see this as a temporary option, I would urge you to visit estates where the majority of people are on government benefits. What you will notice immediately is an atmosphere of tension, depression, disillusionment and despair. What you will see is poverty of income and of aspiration. What you will see is the exact opposite of everything you want for your life!

8. Working for money

The final piece of mis-information delivered to us from our mis-informers is that money is something you should work for. So lets clear this up; every employee is ultimately working for money, however entrepreneurs work to create or to purchase a money-source. Again, we are back to the water and the well. If you give me a cup of water (salary) you will have quenched my thirst for a while. You will also have reinforced my dependency on you. However if you give me a well (wealth), you will have quenched my thirst for life. The difference between employers and employees is that:

1. One works for money while the other works to create a money source.

2. One works for wages while the other works for wealth.

3. One works for a salary while the other works for profits!

Unfortunately this understanding is quite obscure for people who rely on their mis-education for success. The best they can do is work even harder and harder for the person who owns the money source. If they lose a job, they have to go looking for someone else who owns a money-source in order to get some more money. It never even occurs to them that they can own their own money source because they have been mis-educated into a life of job-dependency.

Chapter 5
The Entrepreneurial Mind

He who can, does. He who cannot, teaches.
George Bernard Shaw (1856-1950)
British dramatist, critic, writer.
Maxims for Revolutionists.

As I sit writing this chapter, I am actually in a foreign country where I am the guest speaker at an event. I have been speaking on these and other related subjects and am perhaps quite sensitive to this issue right now. But as I look around me I realise that I am completely surrounded by expressions of the entrepreneurial mind. The flight here, the cars that transported me from the airport to the hotel, the hotel itself with its beautifully landscaped grounds and of course my room with its furniture, its fittings and trimmings. The Mac Book Pro upon which I type and the software that I am using were all created, packaged and sold by an entrepreneurial mind.

Finally, I look out of my window and notice what I think is an exception to the rule; trees and greenery! Then it dawned on me that the trees were clearly planted and arranged as part of an architectural theme to balance out the grey and the green.

You can't escape it; the clothes you wear, the food you eat, the home in which you live are all expressions of the entrepreneurial mind. They were all produced, packaged, promoted, sold and delivered to you by a carefully crafted business system, designed by an entrepreneur. In deed the very progress of humanity and the quality of life that we enjoy today is the result of continuous discovery, invention and improvements that are then translated into products and services.

For example, Thomas Eddison developed the first electric light bulb, right?. Congratulations Thomas! However, the reason why you and I have electric light bulbs in our homes and offices today is that we bought them from a store. Since the days of Eddison, these bulbs have been produced, packaged and promoted at a price. The electric light bulb and indeed electricity itself running through **every home** is the result of entrepreneurial thinking more than it is an expression of scientific progress. If left to a scientist, the electric light bulb would exist in a laboratory at best or in a museum at worst. It is the entrepreneurs who decided to put them into every home!

The same is true of every other invention or technological breakthrough. It is available to us today because it was produced, packaged, priced, promoted and positioned for us by entrepreneurial minds.

Social entrepreneurs

I should make it clear that the entrepreneurial mind is all about creating solutions. This is not always done for profit and nor should it always be. Sometimes it is simply done for the public good. The social enterprise whether it be a rehab, a shelter, an association, a training company or any number of a thousand solutions, is as much an expression of the entrepreneurial mind as is the sky scrapper, the airline and the internet.

The entrepreneurial mind is that freethinking, creative, idealist who believes that dreams were meant to come true. It imagines the un-imaginable, it sees the invisible, it feels the intangible and it expects the impossible. It values imagination more than information, it won't take no for an answer and won't stop searching till it finds a systematic solution to the dilemma at hand.

7 characteristics of a great mind

I cannot fathom why it is that so little attention is given to developing the entrepreneurial mind within youngsters at school, college and university. After all, the entrepreneurial mind is responsible for almost everything that we enjoy and take for granted; from toilet roll to toothpaste. It disturbs me that we may be raising a whole generation who are lacking the three things that can really make them rich, namely; ideas, imagination and initiative!

Through mis-education we have developed great workers, but not great minds! This is a shame because we live in the age of job insecurity and at the same time we are entering the age of entrepreneurial opportunity, where your number one asset is going to be the quality of your ideas.

It has been said that great minds think alike. Quite clearly they don't all think about the same things, but they do all think in the same ways as follows:

1. **Great minds question assumptions** – Breakthroughs, inventions and discoveries in science, medicine and technology are usually the result of someone questioning or challenging the existing assumptions. The truth is that we would never know how far we could go if someone didn't first go too far!

2. **Great minds are future focused** – Small minds are often buried in the past while average minds are usually pre-occupied with the present, but extraordinary minds are always focused on the future. They imagine what could be then they make it their duty to find out how it can be. They are always moving towards a goal and working towards the progressive realisation of a dream.

3. **Great minds reject limitations** – My friend, Dr Stan Harris says that, 'barriers are not meant to hold you back; they are meant to be broken.' As a hall of fame martial artist he knows that wood, ice and concrete can all be broken by human hands if the mind is in the right place. The right place for Dr Stan is beyond the barrier. The martial artist is never trying to break the barrier; instead they are aiming for something beyond

the barrier and that is why they successfully breakthrough the barriers in their way. Great minds can imagine a life beyond the existing barriers. Instead of encouraging people to think within the boundaries of their socio-economic experience, we should nurture the imagination of a life beyond those boundaries.

4. **Great minds are solution orientated** - You will never get a great mind to obsess and whine about a problem. Instead they will focus and concentrate on finding a solution. Solution orientation is the hallmark of a great mind. Solution orientation is the same as asking, seeking and knocking until the answer arrives. My favourite book says, 'everyone who asks receives and whoever seeks will find and to him who knocks it shall be opened.' This is the art of the entrepreneur; creating solutions for people at their point of need!

5. **Great minds ask extraordinary questions:** Extraordinary questions typically begin with What if? Why not? How can we? These questions are designed to induce a state of creativity. For example, the creative scientist would say, what if we put in more of this and less of that? A creative architect might ask, why not build around it? A creative entrepreneur may ask, how can we sell twice as much in half the time? These extraordinary questions awaken a state of extraordinary creativity, which then leads to extraordinary progress.

6. **Great minds place the burden of proof with the sceptics:** Great minds believe that certain things are possible, even though they have no proof of this outside of their gut feeling. However a great mind does not feel obliged to prove their theory to everyone because they are more concerned with manifesting their intentions than they are with winning an argument. Great minds insist that the burden of proof lies with the sceptic. They must prove that it is not possible and while they are busy preparing their case, the great minds will simply get on with the job of making it happen!

7. **Great minds leverage from failure:** Failure is ultimately an education that comes loaded with lessons about what not to do in the future. As such, it is life's way of correcting and perfecting you. Without failure, you would be incapable of achieving success because the greatest lessons you will ever learn about your own success will come from your own failures. The most important things that you need to know about success will be taught to you in the school of hard knocks. The trick is to carry the learning with you into the future, while leaving the pain in the past!

Limited thinking = A limited life!

The objective in mis-education is always to limit your thinking. This is simply because freethinking people are dangerous, difficult to control and difficult to contain. They don't make great workers because their personal standards are often too high, their tolerance for poor conditions is low and their goal is usually to quit the job as soon as possible. These people want more, expect more and demand more from life.

Mis-education serves to strangle the genius, limit the thinking and stifle the creativity out of most people who go through the system. This is done in several ways:

1. By limiting your options – The majority of people come out of the educational system as helpless job-dependents. They have no knowledge, skills or tools for making any money outside of an employer. They leave school, college and university and immediately join the race for jobs. Those who are unsuccessful begin claiming government benefits or they sit at home waiting for the phone call that never comes.

Self-employment is seldom promoted as a viable and affordable alternative to employment, even though the majority of high earners are all self-employed. In this respect people have been grossly mis-informed. **The alternative to employment is not un-employment** (poverty, sitting at home, crime or begging for government help); **it is self-employment!** However, most people haven't even begun to explore this possibility because they have been conditioned to concentrate on landing a good job. So much so that they have no clue how they would make any money without one.

2. By feeding your fears – Much of our education system is based on the fear of unemployment. The suggestion is that if you fail in education, you will become unemployable or that you will at best enter the job market at the lowest levels. Unemployment is then cited as the root cause of poverty, crime, anti-social behaviour, broken families, drug abuse and a host of other dysfunctions.

However, it is the lack of a viable alternative to employment that causes these problems and not the lack of employment itself. It is ultimately job-dependency that should be feared much more than being unable to find a job. The lack of jobs is a fact that we are all going to have to live with. But the lack of an alternative to a job is something we shouldn't have to live with.

What would happen if instead of fearing unemployment, people feared becoming job dependent? The answer is that they would supplement the limited education of the schools with the unlimited success education of mentors.

Thanks to mis-education, most people find out too late that life really offers much more. That is why, people should know from the very earliest stages that there is a sensible and sustainable alternative to employment – i.e. self-employment!

They should also know:

- That self-employment is more likely to deliver financial freedom than is a job.

- That the richest people in the world (who started with little or nothing), did not do well at school and in some cases dropped out.

- That the new economic age has made it more possible for more people to make more money, working for themselves from home, than they could working for somebody else.

- That there are few if any barriers to entry for independent markers and entrepreneurs.

- That there is no shortage of opportunity, and that there are no limits on income for people who play the new game by the new rules.

This sort of education does not produce great workers, because it nullifies the fear of unemployment. It does, however, produce great thinkers by stimulating the entrepreneurial mind and by awakening the creative genius within.

3. By rewarding compliance: Mis-education typically rewards the conformist and punishes the non-conformist. It celebrates those who work hard to achieve job security, whilst it merely tolerates the presence of those who prefer creative expressions like art or inventions. This system of punishment and reward effectively sends out a message to students that says; **concentrate your mental energy on getting a good job because anything else is a waste of time!** However, the sad experience of many is that concentrating on job security has been their biggest and most disappointing waste of time.

This is why so many people are so disillusioned when they leave university with elite qualifications, but are forced to do jobs that are not remotely related to the subjects that they studied so hard for. Worse yet, there are many who cannot land a job at all, and are struggling to pay off a huge student debt. What went wrong here?

These students were misled into putting all their eggs into one basket. They banked all their hopes and dreams on landing a good job! No one told them that the chances of landing a good job are getting slimmer and slimmer everyday. No one told them that with all the will in the world, they may not land a good job. Worse yet, no one told them what to do if the job thing doesn't work out. They were not prepared for the realities of life in the real world. Had someone told them these facts, they may have tapped into their innate entrepreneurial mind to create a series of options, contingencies and alternatives for success.

What would happen if we rewarded creativity, initiative, enterprise and leadership in the same way that we reward academic achievements?

Believe it or not, there are some cultures in the world that require nothing short of self-employment from children who make it through university. 'You must own your own business,' is the mantra they are exposed to on a daily basis. Even if they get a job, they do so as part of their education to gain practical experience before setting up their own business. For these people, business ownership is the point and the prize in education and a job is merely an extension of that education.

Chapter 6

Re-Educating Yourself

"Personal development is your springboard to personal excellence. Ongoing, continuous, non-stop personal development literally assures you that there is no limit to what you can accomplish."

Brian Tracy

The answer to mis-education is re-education. However re-education for job-independence is not readily available in formal institutions. Actually, it is typically available from mentors and teachers who teach from an experience base. People who achieve job independence are usually happy, and in some cases, desperate to share their knowledge and skills with people who want to learn. That's why they write books, produce audios and run mentoring schemes.

Re-education is always self-driven. It isn't compulsory; it is always voluntary. This deals the deathblow to the old theory that your life can be split into learning years and then earning years. Job-independent people are life long learners who continue to invest in their own education. They collect relevant books and audios. They attend relevant seminars and workshops. They employ the relevant mentors and coaches. They are constantly growing their knowledge and skill in the subjects that produce success.

To achieve job-independence you must first become a strategic learner.

Here are ten things that strategic learners know:

1. **Strategic learning is voluntary:** A basic education is compulsory in the developed world. Likewise, many organisations provide compulsory professional development for their staff and key workers. However, strategic learning is an entirely voluntary affair. It is self-directed, self-organised, self-financed, self- motivated and self-supervised learning, based on your personal life and business goals. As such, it is only compulsory for the people who are serious about success.

2. **Strategic learning starts with a goal:** The starting point for strategic self-development is a dream or vision of success. Once you are clear about what success means for you, you can begin to identify the subjects and skills that if mastered will make your success realistic, attainable and inevitable. You cannot begin to design a strategic learning plan until you are clear about what you really want and why those subjects and skills will help you to get more of what you want.

3. **Strategic learning is relevant learning:** Most compulsory education is deemed irrelevant by students because they fail to see how the information will assist them in life or in business. This sense of irrelevance does not happen with strategic learning because you only ever study those subjects and skills that directly relate to your goals, or that assist your efforts for success. This is why we refer to it as strategic learning. Strategy is a military term that basically means a battle plan. Your learning should be part of your personal and professional battle plan, or it is simply a waste of time.

4. **Strategic learning costs money:** Compulsory education is always free and as such tends to be undervalued by the student. Strategic self-development on the other hand is voluntary and must be self financed. This means creating a learning budget, opening a learning account and investing in your own strategic education. It also means being prudent and shopping around for the best products and services in your field. Strategic learners know that learning can be expensive, and that good advice is not cheap. But they also realise that ignorance costs much, much more.

5. **Strategic learning is the ultimate investment:** Money spent on learning is really an investment that yields actual monetary returns. Studies have shown a direct correlation between money spent on

learning and the growth of earnings. The general rule seems to be that if you invest hundreds into your own success education, you get returns in the thousands. Likewise if you invest thousands you get returns in the millions. For example, you may spend thousands on learning how to run a business, but this could eventually yield a return of millions. The general rule is that the more you learn, is the more you earn.

6. **Ignorance is expensive:** Those who spend nothing on personal growth pay a much higher price in the long run in the form of lost opportunities and the lack of professional options. They are usually confined to the bottom of the earning triangle, working in menial or manual jobs and are considered disposable or replaceable by bosses and companies. Whatever dreams they have are really fantasies that are wholly unrealistic and unattainable because they possess neither the knowledge nor the skills necessary to materialise those dreams.

7. **Strategic learning makes your goals realistic:** Any goal is realistic if you acquire the knowledge and develop the skills necessary to achieve it. Whether that goal is to become a billionaire in the next ten years or to transform your body in one year or less. It is all possible if you first find out how it can be done (preferably from those who have already done it) and then develop the skills that are necessary to achieve that result. Knowledge and skills are the only way to turn possibilities into probabilities. The

good news is that you can learn anything that you need to know in order to achieve any goal that you set for yourself.

8. **Strategic learning is learning from the experts:** Anyone can develop a theory based on research however theories based on experience are more reliable, realistic and relevant for strategic learners. Strategic self-developers know that a good mentor can be a more effective lever for business success than would an MBA from a university. Most MBA students do not go on to achieve business success even though their professor and textbooks are academically sound. The problem is that their goal at MBA level is primarily a qualification and not a successful business.

9. **Strategic learning aims for qualities and not qualifications:** The goal in traditional education is a qualification or certificate of competence. The purpose of the certificate is to impress an employer so that you can get a job. Today, many employers realise that a qualification does not equal the qualities needed for the role on offer. Subsequently, interviews have become longer and more stringent as companies look for additional personal skills and attitudes before taking on an employee. This trend is growing, and academic qualifications are steadily decreasing in significance with major employers. Strategic learners on the other hand view success as the ultimate degree and certificate of competence. Their goal is to succeed and this may involve

supplementing their self-directed learning with some formal learning and qualifications, but never involves substituting personal development for formal qualifications.

10. **Learning happens on the exhale:** We inhale information by reading, listening, observing or otherwise taking in new information. However, we exhale it when we explain, share, teach or practise what we have inhaled. True learning occurs as we talk and walk what we have heard and observed. There is no substitute for experience. Learning is accelerated as we dive in and do. This may also mean burning the bridge behind us or removing the safety net beneath us. Strategic learning is not primarily academic in nature; it is practical and must be implemented as part of a real plan to achieve real goals.

Chapter 7

Designing Your Personal Development Plan

The principal goal of education is to create men who are capable of doing new things, not simply of repeating what other generations have done.

Jean Piaget (1896-1980)
Swiss cognitive psychologist.

The most effective personal developers are both strategic and systematic in their approach to learning. This means that they carefully select the subjects and skills they wish to develop based on an analysis of their present and future needs. It also means that their learning is part of an overall plan for success. This method ensures that their learning is consistent with their goals and that it develops them in the areas that matter the most. The following is a seven-step guide to creating a strategic personal development plan.

Conduct a subject and skills audit:

The purpose of this audit is to identify your own knowledge gaps and skills deficiencies. A knowledge gap is the gap between what you currently know and what you need to know in order to achieve your goals, and a skills deficiency is the lack of a necessary ability. If, for example, your goal is to achieve financial freedom over the next ten years, then there are a number of subjects and skills you will need to master, first including; financial literacy, an understanding of services and trends, financial discipline and controls, an advanced financial vocabulary, business skills and more. The more you master these subjects and skills, the more realistic and attainable your goals will become. In fact, you can automatically increase the probability of achieving your goal by achieving mastery of these subjects and skills. On the other hand, you will certainly not achieve financial success if you are financially ignorant or incompetent.

The same rule applies for every other major goal in your life. Great goals become both possible and probable with the mastery of the relevant subjects and skills. It is even safe to say that great achievements in every field are the direct result of subject and skills mastery. Your first job then is to identify which subjects and skills will make your goals realistic, attainable and probable. This will give you the ultimate advantage and is the starting point of an effective personal development plan.

Start by making a list of all the subjects and skills that you think you will need to master in order to achieve your major life and business goals. Once the list is complete, you should start by acquiring a basic or introductory understanding or grasp of each subject. This can be achieved by reading an 'idiots guide.'

At that point you will become aware of your own blind spots. Unlike a knowledge gap, these are the subjects and skills that you need to master but do not currently know that you will need them. They will only become clear once you get started on the basic and introductory level.

For example, when I first started to study speed learning, I thought that all I needed to know was how to speed read. I knew there were a lot of other subjects that I needed to master and that I didn't have much time for study available so I concluded that if I could triple or quadruple my reading speed, I would have mastered a skill that would serve me well. However, as I delved into the field I soon realised that I would also need to boost my memory and find alternative ways of taking notes or recalling vital information. This was my blind spot and I only became aware of it when I began studying in the field. What started out as a speed reading course soon became a speed learning course that incorporated a plethora of other learning techniques that I didn't even know existed. In this respect, your personal development plan will evolve and take you into areas that do not currently appear relevant.

Set goals and targets:

Once you have created your list of necessary subjects and skills, you are ready to set SMART goals. SMART is an acronym that stands for Specific, Measurable, Achievable, Relevant and Time restricted. This is a proven goal setting criteria for quality goal setting. If your goal can be described using all five adjectives then you have effectively set a first class goal.

When setting learning goals you should pay attention to both the **process** and the **product** of learning. This means both what and why you need to learn. The process of learning may involve; reading books, listening to audios, taking courses or attending seminars, workshops and boot camps. However, focusing on the process of learning alone can induce a state of anxiety, which may lead to procrastination. The product of learning on the other hand describes what you will be able to do with your new knowledge and skills. Your new learning will create new opportunities and options for you. These are the products of learning and should equally form part of your goal setting exercise.

If for example you want to learn Spanish, you may choose to do an evening course or perhaps purchase an audio learning programme on the subject. However this only describes the process of learning Spanish. The fact is that learning to speak Spanish fluently will open up a new world of opportunities, options and possibilities for you. It may open up a Spanish speaking market to your products and services or it may give you an opportunity to immigrate and start a new life in a Spanish speaking country. The big question here is; what is it about speaking Spanish that really excites you? This is the product or result of learning Spanish. Your learning goals should always emphasise the product of learning in terms of the new opportunities or options that you are really seeking to develop. In this respect they are really learning outcomes.

Insert stages and phases:

Once you are clear about the outcomes you envisage from learning, you should develop a Measurable Action Plan (MAP) in three definite stages. The stages, for ease of memory, each begin with the letter R. First is the resource stage. This means, identifying, locating and purchasing the books and audios needed to close your knowledge gaps or to achieve subject mastery. You should likewise identify, locate and enrol in any courses, seminars, workshops, mentoring programmes or boot-camps that you need in order to make up for your skills deficiencies. The same rule applies to websites, blogs, associations and publications that form part of your personal development plan. You should identify, locate and subscribe to them during the resource stage of your MAP. The resource stage also involves creating and setting aside a learning budget. Instead of looking for the money when the opportunities emerge, you should predetermine to spend a percentage of your income on learning and then literally put the money aside each month. You should have a clear idea of how much your learning will cost and then simply go to work on saving or raising that money.

The second stage is the rhythm stage. This means setting aside time each week to study and practise your subjects and skills. No one can get fit by working out occasionally, even if they spend hours in the gym at a time. Fitness is the result of routines and rhythm. Mental fitness is no different. You literally have to get into the rhythm and groove of learning habitually. There are elements of your plan that should be practised daily like reading and listening to audios. Other elements will be practised weekly like courses and rehearsals. Others yet will become monthly, quarterly or even annual activities, like boot-camps, or seminars. The key is to create a rhythm by predetermining when, where and how you will pursue mastery in your field. This involves time management which is really the management of priorities such that your high value tasks are completed before your lower value tasks begin. Finding time to learn can be difficult if not impossible. You will therefore have to make it by getting up earlier, utilising travel time and scaling down on your low value activities like TV, internet surfing, excessive socialising and meaningless telephone conversations.

The final stage in your MAP is the results. This describes the level of competence or mastery that you wish to attain. All learning occurs on four levels based on various degrees of competence. It starts with an **'unconscious incompetence.'** These are your knowledge gaps and blind spots. But once you have designed a personal development plan you will have moved up to the next level which is often referred to as the **'conscious incompetence.'** At this point you at least know the subjects and skills that would give you the edge and advantage in life and business. You will also have embarked on a journey to achieve competence and even mastery in these areas. On that journey you will acquire new knowledge and skills but they will at first seem difficult and un-natural because they will require lots of conscious effort in order to make them work for you. This is the level known as **'conscious competence.'** Everyone who can drive a car has experienced this. Even after you pass your test, the driving experience is still difficult and daunting. Eventually however, your new skills pass into the realm of unconscious competence, where you don't even have to think about how to drive, because it has become natural and instinctive. On this level, driving becomes fun and the anxiety dissipates.

The results stage of your plan then should list the subjects and skills that you wish to develop into unconscious competences as a result of learning. These are not the same as the overall learning outcomes described in your goal setting exercise. Those outcomes describe what you will be able to do with your skills in terms of seizing new opportunities and options in life and business. Stage three results on the other hand, describe the skills you wish to master themselves, and not so much what you will do with them. For example, your overall aim may be to do business in a Spanish speaking country. If this is the case, then stage three of your personal development plan should say, I want to be able to conduct a fluent conversation in Spanish.

The key to staging your plan is to attach realistic yet demanding time frames around each stage so that each phase comes complete with a start and finish date. By time restricting your plan, you will lock yourself into action mode. For example, you may give one month to stage 1 and then 6 months to stage 2 and then a further 3 months to stage 3. The time allocated will vary depending on the resources available, the complexity of the subject matter and the level of competence that you wish to attain. It is possible to achieve competence in a given area in just one month of reading or practise however true mastery occurs with a commitment to continuous and never ending improvement.

Create milestones and measurements:

Regular self-assessments are a critical component in your personal development plan. Without them you may lose your own location i.e. where you are in relation to where you are meant to be. This is the difference between where you think you are in the plan and where you really are. If, for example you think that you are making progress when in fact you are not, then you will become frustrated and even disillusioned with personal development. Likewise if you think that you are not making real progress, you may lose momentum even if in reality you are right on track. The only way to accurately locate yourself in personal development is to incorporate milestones and measurements into your plan. This means breaking down each stage into definite steps. Of course each stage is a milestone in and of itself, however each stage may take months and in some cases, years to complete. You should therefore breakdown each stage into bite size strategic steps. This way you can count and monitor the steps that you are taking in the direction of your desired outcomes.

For example, stage 1 in your PDP is the resource stage. This will inevitably involve some research, costing and expenditure. Each of these strategic steps constitutes a milestone in your plan and should be regarded as such. With each milestone reached, you should derive a sense of satisfaction and success because it means that you are now one strategic step closer to your ultimate destination. Milestones enable you to monitor and measure your progress. Without them, self-assessments don't work.

Incorporating milestones as performance indicators into your personal development plan is a matter of listing the strategic steps that you must take in each stage of your plan and then simply attaching a deadline to it. Each step should have a date on it. This way you will know where you should be at any given time and whether or not you need to accelerate your learning in order to meet your targets.

Create a circle of accountability:

The final key to designing a personal development plan is to share it with two or three people that you both trust and admire. Let them know what you are planning to do and ask them to review your plan. Invite comments, questions and suggestions about the plan and about your own aims and objectives. This may prove extremely valuable as they may be able to spot inconsistencies and goal conflicts that could later emerge to derail your dreams. You may become blind to these glitches because of an obsession with the outcomes or simply because of over familiarity with the plan. It is a well known fact that the author of a work tends to see what they meant to write and not what they actually did write. That is why editors who are not emotionally attached to the project will usually pick up on mistakes that the author simply could not see.

Beyond critiquing the plan, your circle of accountability will prove to be a priceless source of motivation because going back or slacking up may cause you to lose face with people that you trust and admire. Everyone wants to be respected by the people that they respect. Sharing your plans therefore with a respected few is a way of burning the bridges behind you. Everytime they ask how you are doing, you will want to say, I am making progress.

Chapter 8

Building Your Success Library

"Most of the important things in the world have been accomplished by people who have kept on trying when there seemed to be no hope at all."

Dale Carnegie

Success is a matter of mental chemistry. It involves mixing your own ideas with the ideas of leading experts and outstanding achievers in order to achieve extraordinary intelligence in your field. Napoleon Hill, author of the best selling 'Think and Grow Rich' had the privilege of interviewing and shadowing over 500 of the most successful people of his day. He documented his research and authored what some consider to be the most comprehensive science of success. He identified seventeen laws of success and taught that success was the result of co-operating with those laws. All of his laws were mental laws and involved developing a state of mind that mirrored the circumstances desired.

One of Napoleon Hill's major discoveries was what he called super intelligence. He found that outstanding people had access to super intelligence and that this was primarily the result of two or more minds harmoniously working together to achieve a goal. He claimed that the mental chemistry of two or more minds, united in their determination to achieve a definite purpose, produced a master -mind that possessed super-intelligence. From that super-intelligence came the ideas, solutions, innovations, ingenuity and creativity that characterised the most successful people of his day.

Today it is easier than ever to access the super intelligence of collective thoughts because those collective thoughts are readily available for the price of a book. As you set about collecting and absorbing the philosophies and strategies of leading experts and outstanding achievers, you will begin to exhibit extraordinary intelligence in that field. Where does extraordinary intelligence come from anyway? The answer is that it is the result of learning from your own and other peoples experiences.

In this respect, no one is self made. We are all the product of other people's insights and inputs. There is really no such thing as a self-made millionaire. Although the term is convenient for describing the people who started with nothing and went on to achieve millionaire status, it is misleading if it is understood to mean that they achieved millionaire status without the insights and inputs of other people. The truth is that we are all the products of learning; nothing more and nothing less!

If this is true, then you will not succeed without a success library. This is your collection of educational books, audios, articles, reports, publications and videos/DVD's. Although your library will start small, it will eventually become large. Space won't become a problem unless you don't read or study them. If you do read them, you will develop extraordinary intelligence and as a result, an extraordinary income. You will almost certainly move premises into your dream home with its own purpose built library.

Here are ten keys to developing your own success library:

1. **Get an account with Amazon or other reputable retailers.** Unless you enjoy going to book shops you should start by opening an account with an online retailer so that you can order books and audio books from home. These websites come complete with powerful search engines so that you can search by topic, author, titles, publisher or the best sellers list. They are also able to recommend books of a similar nature to the ones you select or that other buyers also bought on your topic. In addition to this, books are usually discounted and used copies can often be purchased at a fraction of the price. Online retailers will always have a larger selection than would a store and can often source books that are out of print.

2. **Start with a list of topics:** You should make a list of the topics that interest you or that would best serve your personal and professional goals. These are typically non-fiction, self-help, business, leadership, careers, management, biographic, history, popular psychology and skills based books. These are the sections most frequented by personal developers in book stores. Once you have identified your

own knowledge gaps and skill deficiencies, you should include these on your list of topics. Pay special attention to your strengths when developing your list of topics in a way that develops your strengths more so than your weaknesses.

3. **Use the five book rule:** If you read and understand five books written by leading experts on a given subject, you will become an authority on that subject. Remember that if the book is written by experts; it is more than a book. It is the result of a life time of experience and research. Make it your goal then to purchase five books by internationally acclaimed authors on each subject you have selected. There is no need to buy them all at once, as this may not be economically feasible. One at a time will do. The basic rule is that if you read five books on the subjects or skills you wish to develop than you will have all the tools and techniques you need in order to achieve a high level of competence in that field. Achieving expertise or mastery in a subject or skill will take much more reading as well as years of implementation and experience. It is estimated that the experts have read between two and five hundred or more books in their field. Now that is a big success library.

4. **Start with the idiots guide:** The idiots guide and, other beginners guides, are an excellent resource for personal developers An idiots guide exists on virtually any subject that you can imagine. Simply use your

online retailer to search for an idiots guide or a 'for dummies' guide on the subjects of your choice. These authors assume that the reader knows absolutely nothing about the subject matter at hand and thereby manage to break down very complex subjects into bite size chunks, written in simple, everyday language. It is a mistake to assume that idiots guides are not substantial or that they are somehow inadequate. Quite to the contrary, they are often so comprehensive that they can give the reader a sense of mastery. The difference is that they are designed for ease of reading and quick comprehension.

5. **Connect with the authors:** Best selling authors usually have websites offering additional learning materials in the form of audio programs, e-news, reports, articles, seminars and boot camps that further explain and support the core concepts and philosophies expressed in their books. If a particular author resonates with you, then connect with them online to see if you can gain additional insight on their subject matter expertise. This material is often not available from other retailers and must be purchased direct from the author.

6. **Use executive summaries:** Many boom clubs and retailers offer quick read summaries of best selling non-fiction books. These booklets can be read in one sitting and often successfully summarise the main ideas contained in the book. Although the summary is intended to be an appetiser

for the book, it can sometimes serve as a substitute for it.

7. **Utilise the power of audio:** Most non-fiction; self-help books are readily available in mp3 format. They can be purchased or downloaded to your mp3 player and carried with you for listening during travel time. In addition to this, the authors often publish recorded seminars and audio programs that are available from their websites. They may also broadcast podcasts and tele-conferences. In fact, many of America's reputable universities now deliver whole courses for free from the iTunes store. iTunes is a free media organiser that can be downloaded from the Apple store online. Once downloaded you can access the iTunes store and make use of hours and hours of university lectures and academic discussions.

8. **Use e-books and web articles:** When it comes to e-books and web articles, cheap doesn't mean rubbish. E-books are cheap and most articles or reports are free to download from the internet. The key is to print them off or to file them electronically so that they can be easily retrieved.

9. **Utilise the power of video/DVD's:** Documentaries and educational programs should form part of your success library. So should video podcasts. Again, these can be purchased from your online retailer or from the authors own website.

10. Create an effective filing system: Nothing is worse than not being able to find material that you need when you need it most. Books should be shelved by topic or by author, depending on what works for you. Articles should be filed in durable folders that are clearly labelled and stored in an appropriate space. Audio programmes should be shelved together but grouped according to subject or author. Likewise, DVD's should be kept together but grouped by subject. Digital books and articles should also be filed in clearly marked folders and backed up so that they can be easily retrieved. Finally, you should keep an inventory of all items in your success library including titles, authors, publishers and price. If possible keep all receipts and include your library in your home contents insurance against fire or theft.

Chapter 9

Sustained Momentum

"Look at a day when you are supremely satisfied at the end. It's not a day when you lounge around doing nothing; it's when you've had everything to do, and you've done it."

Margaret Thatcher

No one can get fit by occasionally visiting the gym in their spare time. This is not only a waste of time but may also produce more harm in the long term. To see and sustain lasting results you have to regiment your workouts by eating the right foods and working with a trainer each week. Fitness then is the result of a routine and the same is true of mental fitness. You cannot seriously develop your mental capacity by occasionally reading a book or listening to an audio. The only way to see and sustain meaningful results in this area is to create a learning routine that makes personal development a major priority and a daily habit.

This at first may seem difficult, however once you get over the initial struggle, the law of momentum will take over and make your learning routine a natural and pleasurable part of your everyday life. Your goal in personal development is to achieve momentum. This occurs when your learning routine takes on a life and energy of its own. Instead of you being the driving force behind it, it will become the driving force behind your success. The following is a guide to achieving and sustaining momentum in learning.

1. **Get started** – None of the tools and techniques offered in this programme will make you a strategic learner until you take action and get started. This is the most difficult step in personal development because it is often loaded with anxiety and doubts. The best way to dispel these doubts and fears is to simply take the first step no matter how small it is. Simply pull out a piece of paper and write answers to the following questions: What would success mean for me? Which subjects and skills if mastered would secure the success that I envisage? Once you have identified the subjects and skills that would make your success realistic and attainable, you should go about sourcing one book or audio programme on each of those subjects. Give yourself one month to explore each subject until you grasp the basic ideas and techniques offered. This simple four part process will get you started as a strategic learner.

2. **Develop a master mind alliance** – create a network of two or three other's who share a similar success wish to you. Agree to meet with them either in person, online or on the phone at least once per week to share ideas and to discuss what you have been

learning. Your discussions will not only serve to motivate you but the mental chemistry between the group will also create a collective mind with the capacity to solve problems and to generate ideas that you could not have come up with on your own. Your weekly meetings will also allow you to exhale your learning. True learning does not occur on the inhale of new ideas but rather when we exhale them through teaching, sharing, explaining or doing something new. For example, it may be your goal to achieve mastery of the subject and skills necessary to become an expert marketer. Marketing is your subject and with it comes a host of new skills to learn and to master. As part of your plan, you may be reading several books by experts or listening to audios by millionaire marketers. Simply use your master mind meeting to exhale what you have been reading. You can do this by sharing or explaining a concept in marketing that you have just learned. Finally, your master mind group will serve as a circle of accountability around your learning goals. You should share your goals and strategy with the group so that they too can monitor and measure your progress.

3. **Create a learning budget** – There is a direct correlation between the amount of money you spend on personal development and the amount of money you earn. The general rule is that the more you learn, the more you will earn. This means that to earn more you must first learn more. In this respect money spent on learning is really an investment that

yields actual monetary returns in addition to its other benefits. Strategic learners know that every penny they spend on learning will produce a return on that investment and so they look forward to their next purchase with glee. Books, audio programmes, seminars and boot camps all cost money. That money should be factored into your budget so that each month a certain amount is put aside for personal development. A good starting point is 10%. Anyone who spends 10% of their income on personal growth can expect to double their income in ten months or less. The best way to do this is to open a separate learning account and then to deposit 10% of your income into it each month. All of your spending on learning products should then come from that account.

4. **Focus on your true goals** – strategic learning is all about mastering the subjects and skills that will secure the success that you envisage for yourself. Your true goal then is success, and learning is simply a means to that end. In this respect, the process of learning involves study but the product of learning is success. You can sustain your momentum by focusing on the product of learning i.e. what you will be able to do with your new knowledge and skills. Knowledge and skills will open doors for you, create opportunities for you and deliver multiple options to you. By regularly reminding yourself of those opportunities you can both create and sustain your learning momentum.

5. **Reward yourself** – Your strategic learning plan should come complete with goals and outcomes, stages and phases, milestones and measurements, resources and rewards. Each stage in your plan is worth celebrating so decide at the beginning what you will do to treat yourself as you complete each stage. Your rewards need not be expensive but they should be memorable and thoroughly enjoyable.

6. **Take it to the next level** – After several months of learning you may find that you reach a plateaux or that you begin to stagnate. This is caused by a growing sense of irrelevance or the feeling that you are not making progress. Its symptoms include a loss of enthusiasm, purpose and energy. If this happens, don't panic, all is not lost. It usually means that your routine is lacking the challenge that it did at first or that it is no longer stretching you. It may also means that the learning has lost its strategic edge by becoming irrelevant to your current situation or to your future goals. When this occurs, you should raise the bar by taking your learning to the next level. Simply review your learning plan to see if the subjects are still relevant to your goals. Once the subjects are in place you should up the anti by increasing the pace of learning. For example: instead of one book per month, resolve to read two or more. Likewise, you can create for yourself tasks, assignments or projects that demand greater comprehension or more skill in that area. By raising the bar, you will reignite your passion for success and restore to yourself the joy of learning.

7. **Realise that you are in a race** – we are in a learning race in which the fastest learners are the biggest earners. New technologies, new markets, new products, new services and ever increasing consumer choice has created an economic race in which companies must either catch up or get left behind. This means that the most valuable asset in today's organisation is the fast learner. Fast learners can grasp new ideas, use new technologies, develop new skills and manage change more easily than would a slow learner. Those who learn slowly or who avoid learning altogether can only slow the organisation down because an organisation can move no faster than its directors and key workers. The fact is that slow learners will eventually find themselves out of a job because they constitute big liabilities for organisations that are competing to win. Whatever you are aiming for in life, remember that thousands if not millions of people are also aiming for it too. If you want to be on top of your game, then waste no time in acquiring the knowledge and skills that will take you to the top.

8. **Play to win** – You should aim to be in the top 10% of the most productive and prosperous people in your field or get out of the field all together, for the following reasons:

• The 90/10 rule says that 90% of the industry is controlled by only 10% of the people in it. These are the best in the business who have achieved mastery of the subjects and skills necessary to succeed.

- 90% of the rewards are reserved for the top 10%. In every industry sector, there is an earnings triangle in which the majority of people are at the bottom and only a small minority are at the top. Those on the lower levels have to compete with each other over only 10% of the money available in that sector whilst the top 10% get to enjoy 90% of the income generated by the industry.

- Whatever field you go into, the same rule will apply. Those who change career because they are not earning enough or because they have little time for themselves will soon discover that no one in the bottom 90% of any industry is earning enough or has any time for themselves. The problem is not the industry but rather your position in it. There are few rewards, little security and no freedom for the bottom 90% in any field of business. This is why you should play to win or get out of the game altogether. You should aim for the top or find another mountain. You should be the best or relinquish the benefits.

The good news is that there is a direct correlation between the earnings triangle and the learning triangle. Those at the bottom of the ET have had a compulsory basic education while those in the middle have participated in compulsory professional development. Those at the top are addicted to voluntary, strategic learning.

www.thehomebusinessacademy.com

Chapter 10

Business made simple

Understand that you need to sell you and your ideas in order to advance your career, gain more respect, and increase your success, influence and income.

Jay Abraham

Business is not financial science, it's about trading.. buying and selling. It's about creating a product or service so good that people will pay for it.

Anita Roddick

If you go to a bookstore and look in the business section, you'll find all sorts of books on everything from business strategy and systems to organisational culture, management, leadership, innovation and more. Anyone reviewing these sections could easily conclude that business is both complicated and difficult. However, nothing could be further from the truth. Business is simple when you understand what real business is. I'm not suggesting that these other subjects are not important or that the information in those books is not useful. I am suggesting that business itself is quite simple, easy to understand and easy to undertake when you strip it down to its core.

Business processes, systems and structures are all ancillary to the business. They become necessary as the business grows but must never be confused with the business itself. The things we do to support and grow our businesses shouldn't be confused with or construed as the actual act of business. A failure to recognise this distinction is in fact one of the leading causes of business failure. When companies take their eye off the ball; spending more time and money on appearances and processes, than on the actual transaction of business they will inevitably fail.

This error is the fruit of traditional business thinking. When a company has a huge bank overdraft facility, it can usually afford to do everything except the business itself. However in these troubled times when credit is less available, companies are going to have to knuckle down and get back to business. This chapter is designed to simplify the act of doing business so that you will see how quickly you can go into business yourself.

What is business?

When you strip business down to its core function, you will see that it is simply the act of trading or exchanging value (in the form of goods or services) for money. Business is fundamentally a transaction in which goods and services are exchanged for money or for goods and services of equivalent value. No matter how valuable your goods or services, you are not in business until they are exchanged for money. For example, you may own a restaurant and cook the tastiest meals, but until someone buys a meal, there is no business in progress. Likewise you may produce the best music in the world but until it is exchanged for money, you are not in the music business. In this respect the real business occurs at the point of a sale.

Companies who lose sight of this simple fact, end up focusing their efforts on everything but sales. They see sales as a function of the business along side other functions like admin and management, instead of seeing it as the business itself. In this respect they fail to prioritise the customer and instead begin prioritising their own organisation.

Real business is sales and without a sale there is no business in progress. Sales is both the purpose and the point in business. It is the great objective and the consummation of every other business function. Everything else in business falls or rises on sales because without a sale it was all a waste of time and money. Production, admin, premises, staff, management, tech support, customer services and market research are all about sales. Likewise innovation, leadership, PR, branding and the rest are all justified by sales.

I know that some of you business experts may disagree. You may feel that the objective in business is profits or customer satisfaction. Maybe you think it is to meet needs or fill a gap in the market. So let me make this clear; your objective in business should not be confused with the business itself. The business itself is transacted at the point of a sale. It happens when goods and services are exchanged for money. This single act is responsible for your profits, your customers, your significance and your market share. In fact, without a customer (sale) you are not in business no matter how strong your brand, your team, your product offering or your campaign.

This simple truth is great news for ordinary people who are trapped in the 9-5 grind. Because it means that you can go into business and make some additional money immediately. All you need to do is exchange something for money. It could be an item, a service, or some information.

Try it! Look around you now and identify something of value that you would be happy to sell. You may need to pop into the garage or the cupboard to do this. Once you've found something that you are happy to lose, make a short list of people you know who might be interested in having it. Then call each one of them using the following script: Hi, just wanted to let you know that I'm getting rid of my...............if you're interested you can have it for $?

If you don't want to make the phone calls, then just send out an email to family and friends with a similar message.

If the price is right, you will no doubt generate a sale within one hour. Can I prove it? Yes! Millions are making money on eBay and craigslist every-day. These are auction web sites where people can advertise their goods for free and then sell them to the highest bidder. The same phenomenon occurs at 'car boot' sales in England. These are ordinary people exchanging their odds and ends for money.

Making Money!

There is only one legal way to make money on planet earth; that is **to exchange goods or services for it.** Even if you are employed, your employer pays you in exchange for your services rendered. You in turn, help your employer to get more money in exchange for goods or services sold by the company.

The opposite is also true; you only ever give your money to others in exchange for goods or services. In this respect **money is simply a medium of exchange.** In fact, none of us really wants more money! What we really want are the things that we can exchange it for. Apart from its power of exchange it is nothing more than pieces of pretty paper or digits on a screen. It is the power of exchange that gives money its value.

What you really want is the things that money can buy. This is exactly how all consumers think. When they make money, they immediately begin thinking of all the things they can do with it. They think of things they can avoid and of things they can obtain with money. They start spending it in their minds. Its value is in direct proportion to the things they can buy with it. Let me ask you a question, which would you rather have; a million Zimbabwe dollars, or a thousand American dollars? I know the answer, but why? Because a thousand American dollars can buy more than a million Zimbabwe dollars!

Money was made to move! It is nothing more than purchasing power. Stagnant money is worthless. It is a pile of paper, until you realise and activate its 'power of exchange.' Even if you put it in a bank, the bank will rent it out in exchange for more money. This is why money is sometimes referred to as 'liquid,' because it flows in one of two directions:

1. **Away from you** – This occurs when you purchase things that depreciate in value or that costs more to maintain than it can be sold for or that are beyond your financial

means. These liabilities take money away from you and will ultimately limit your purchasing power.

2. **Towards you** – This occurs when you offer goods or services in exchange for money. If the goods or services are in demand and are marketed well, consumers will give you money in exchange for them.

Turning the tide

If you are going to successfully turn the tide and get money flowing towards you, you will have to think of something you can sell. Many people go wrong at this point. They start looking for something to sell with their 'sellers' spectacles on, instead of the 'buyers' spectacles. Here's what they do:

'They start thinking about products and services that they would like to sell for one reason or another.'

This is a mistake because research and experience has proven that sellers live and think in a different world than do buyers and that what impresses the seller may mean nothing to the buyer. Consumers view products and advertising in a completely different way than do companies and sales people. These two perspectives are often so far apart that the one is alien to the other, as follows:

Each group has its own paradigm, language and values as follows:

1. **Consumer paradigm:** The number one thought going through the mind of a consumer is, **'What's in it for me?'** Consumers are selfish,

merciless and suspicious of all advertising. They want more for less, they want it now and they want to retain total control even after the purchase! They do not care about you or your brand or your business, they only care about themselves!

2. **Consumer language:** Consumers describe products in terms of benefits to themselves.

3. **Consumer values:** Consumers value results and outcomes. They purchase products as a means to an end and want to know if your products will deliver the end result they are looking for.

On the other hand is the seller as follows:

1. **The seller's paradigm:** This is how sellers think: We have a good product, consumers need it and they are crazy if they don't buy it!

2. **Seller language:** Sellers describe their products in terms of their features, qualities and standards; colour, shape, size, materials, power, specifications etc. They often use trade lingo when talking to customers or when advertising as though they are speaking to colleagues.

3. **Seller values:** Sellers typically value their own brand, their own aspirations and their own incomes. Customers are simply a means to an end.

Two boxes

These two paradigms are like two boxes in which two groups live. Before you go looking for something to sell, you should get out of the sellers box and into the buyers box. Here's what you should do:

Instead of asking what can I sell? You should ask, 'what do consumers want to buy?' Instead of asking what should I sell? You should ask, 'what are people buying?'

When you jump into the consumer box, you will be able to hear the conversation going on in the minds of consumers. Listen carefully until you can work out their:

1. Issues
2. Concerns
3. Aspirations
4. Dreams
5. Fears
6. Desires
7. Doubts
8. Goals

These things will give you a clue as to what consumers want and therefore what you should sell.

When thinking of something to sell,

- Make sure that it plugs into the issues and aspirations of your consumers.

- Make sure that it is already in demand

- Make sure that it fits the customer's (self-seeking) paradigm

- Make sure that it speaks the customers (benefits-based) language

- Make sure that it promises an outcome that is desirable to your customer.

The master skill:

Nothing is more obvious in life than sales. Look around you? Virtually everything you can physically see right now was produced then marketed and sold for money at some point. In addition to this, human beings are constantly engaged in selling themselves, their ideas and their plans to others. Of course most of these are not monetary transactions but the principle remains the same. We are constantly asking others to buy into us. It happens on a date, at a job interview, with friends and in a hundred other life circumstances. Babies and toddlers do it and so do parents. It is both natural and instinctive to sell.

Most of us are comfortable selling our points of view or selling ourselves to others but haven't yet learned to take it one step further to selling goods and services for money. This is partly because of the stigma attached to sales people as pushy, arrogant and unethical.

No one wants to be avoided by good people and no one wants to be labelled with the above. Undoubtedly some sales people have let down the rest by resorting to cowboy tactics and misrepresentation. However this does not change the fact that sales is the only business there is. One way to overcome the stigma is to consider yourself a consultant, an advisor or an educator. Sales professionals wear many labels to today, but when you strip their function down to its core, they are in the business of sales. In this respect; sales is an honourable, noble and classy profession. It is the only profession that exists.

There would be no professional sports without sales, no concerts or theatres without sales, no film and cinema without sales, no holidays or homes without sales, no leisure or luxuries without sales and no recreation and restaurants without it. Don't knock it and don't buy into the idea that it is some how beneath you. It is not just the oldest profession in the world; it is the only profession in the world!

If you learn how to sell, you will secure your income for life. If you learn how to sell, you'll never go out of business. If you learn how to sell, you will be in demand by every type of business on earth. Going into business is as easy as learning how to sell.

The greater the financial impact of a sale; the more skill you will need to develop in order to secure it. Selling something for $2000.00 requires a more advanced selling strategy and understanding of consumer psychology than would selling an item for $20.00. Likewise if you are selling something for $200,000 you will have to become a bit more commercially sophisticated than would someone who sells items for $2000.00. People who sell yachts employ a different strategy than do people who sell peanuts, however the principles are the same.

www.thehomebusinessacademy.com

Chapter 11

Marketing made simple

No matter what your product is, you are ultimately in the education business. Your customers need to be constantly educated about the many advantages of doing business with you, trained to use your products more effectively, and taught how to make never-ending improvement in their lives.

Robert G Allen

If you're attacking your market from multiple positions and your competition isn't, you have all the advantage and it will show up in your increased success and income.

Jay Abraham

So what is your prospective customer thinking right now? What are their issues and their concerns? The answer is that it all depends on which area of their life you are considering.

There are 8 major concerns of people living in the free world as follows:

1. **Spirituality:** This includes religion, philosophy, belief systems, guidance, inner peace,

religious education, meditation, prayer and more.

2. **Health and fitness:** This includes medical issues, weight loss, physical fitness, mental health, wellness, nutrition and more

3. **Love and family:** This includes singles, dating, marriage, weddings, children, home improvements, schooling and more.

4. **Career:** This includes employment, career change, redundancy, rights, self-employment, business ownership and more.

5. **Personal finances:** This includes asset protection, wealth creation, debt, litigation, bankruptcy, savings, mortgages, financial services and more.

6. **Social lifestyle:** This includes entertainment, friendships, hobbies, leisure, travel, music, social networking, nightlife and more.

7. **Personal development:** This includes self-education, reading, skills development, professional development, new languages, learning and growing and more.

8. **Contribution:** This includes charitable causes, public services, politics, associations, action groups, lobbying, fundraising and more.

These are the eight major concerns for people living in the free world.

- They also constitute eight markets for independent entrepreneurs.

- Each of these eight markets houses hundreds of niche markets for particular products or services. i.e the careers market, or the personal development market. I call these the eight 'macro-niche markets!'

- Each macro niche market houses thousands of micro niche markets for smart entrepreneurs. A micro niche is a niche within a niche.

For example, the personal development market houses niche markets for various forms of success education. However within these markets there is a micro niche for success classics. i.e. success literature that is over 50 years old.

Likewise the **lifestyle market** houses the **'hobbies niche.'** However within this niche is the **'model train micro-niche.'**

Stephen Pierce says, 'if you want to go broke, market to all the folk but if you want to get rich, then market to a niche.' (Pronounced 'nitch' in America)

The main thing to remember about any niche market is that consumers are never looking for products or services;

- They are looking for outcomes and results
- They are looking for a bargain
- They are looking for a risk free purchase (money back guarantee)
- They are looking for customer service

This way of thinking is critical for smart marketers who must decide what they are going to sell. If you answer this question in the customer's box, you are more likely to pick a niche that works.

Simply put yourself in the customer's shoes by jumping into one of the eight macro-nice markets and then ask yourself, what do I want to buy right now and why? Imagine that you are a single parent then ask yourself, what do I want to buy right now? Do the same for someone who is at risk of losing their job or for someone who is struggling to lose weight.

Thinking from the customers perspective is a critical skill for independent marketers. That is why:

- You should work with a niche that you can relate to

- You should work with a niche that you have some knowledge of

- You should thoroughly research the niche to improve your knowledge of it

- You should study the niche before sourcing a product

- You should obtain any available data about your niche before deciding to sell to it

- You should find what people want (outcomes and results) in this field, so that you will know what to sell.

Why niche marketing works

The high street does not typically cater for special interests. It is designed for volume and so restricts its shop floors to items with broad appeal. People with special interests have to search online for the few suppliers who can meet their specific requirements. This is great news for independent entrepreneurs who are poised to meet the needs of macro and micro niche markets. Special needs require specialist services.

Your self-concept:

To be an effective independent marketer you must learn to see yourself as a representative, a spokes-person and an advocate for your niche. There is an old and well-established war between the supply side of the market and the demand side as consumers have grown to mistrust companies and sales people. Bad sales people typically represent their companies and products but independent marketers typically represent their customers.

Representing your customers means:

- Appreciating their needs (in that area of their life)

- Appreciating their frustrations with existing products

- Appreciating their aspirations – the outcomes, results and objectives they envisage

- Appreciate their scepticism – mistrust of amazing offers!

If you can demonstrate an appreciation of your customers needs, frustrations, aspirations and scepticism, in your marketing documents, you will achieve what I call 'customer rapport.' Rapport could best be described as two people dancing to the same beat. When it is present; defences come down and trust goes up.

This is why it is so critical that you research your market thoroughly so that you can acquaint yourself with consumer issues. Here's what you do:

- Join reputable online forums or discussions on your subject

- Subscribe to online newsletters on this subject

- Download any free e-books on your subject

- Try out your competitors to see what frustrates you

- Interview anyone you know who has a frustration in this area.

- Make a list of the 10 most common frustrations that people face in this area

- Find out how many searches are done per month around the key words in your niche market using Google ad words.

A conflict of interests!

Bad sales people often experience a conflict of interests when pushing a product on customers that they neither want nor need. Since their chief aim is to sell the product and earn commissions, their approach can be intrusive. Authentic marketers on the other hand experience no such conflict because their chief aim is to satisfy, delight and even amaze their customers. They see themselves as customer representatives whose job it is to promote the best solutions for their customers needs. Their loyalties lie with the customer and not with their products.

In addition to this, when it comes to Internet marketing; pushy sales tactics don't work because the customer has the power to silence you with the click of a mouse. They will only ever keep reading your website if you can achieve **'customer rapport.'**

In summary:

- There are eight areas of concern for people living in the free world. These eight constitute macro niche markets filled with buyers who have special interests.

- Each of these eight houses hundreds of regular niche markets, which in turn house thousands of micro-niche markets filled with consumers of products not readily available in the high street

- Authentic marketers represent the interests of their niche market by sourcing products and services that genuinely meet or surpass consumer expectations

- If a particular niche market resonates with you, you should first research the market thoroughly to see if it is viable and so that you can achieve customer rapport in your marketing documents by demonstrating an advanced appreciation of your customers needs, frustrations, aspirations and scepticisms.

A marketing metaphor

This metaphor is designed for home-based entrepreneurs who use the internet as their chief marketing tool.

Modern marketing is like fishing with a boat, a line, a hook and of course some bait. The ocean is the world-wide web complete with billions of fish – consumers.

Your boat is your business that sails out on the ocean. Your bait is the irresistible offer made by your **list-building** website (I'll explain this a little later). Once a consumer accepts your irresistible free or low cost offer, they have bitten your bait and have become hooked (part of your list).

The line is your sales process. Your job is to draw in those who are already hooked and not to try and draw in anyone that is not already hooked.

Bigger brands can go fishing with a net, but independent marketers must bait, hook and draw customers into the exchange of value for money. The important lessons here are that:

- You must bring your boat (business) to where people are and not wait for them to come to you.

- You must first throw your baited hook (list-building website with its irresistible offer) into the ocean before you can expect to catch any fish.

- You need to hook them before you can draw them, through the sales process, into your business!

Seven Marketing secrets:

Marketing secret 1 – stop trying to boil the ocean!

Authentic marketers are not trying to market their products to the whole world. They are only interested in marketing to a list of pre-qualified prospects. Pre-qualified prospects are people who:

o   Want the products
o   Can afford the products

You can use the Internet to prequalify prospects. The golden rule is; 'he that is faithful in little is faithful also in much'. This means that those who spend a little with you are most likely to spend more.

Marketing secret 2 – Only market to your list

Independent marketers do not market products and services to the world; they only market their goods to their unique mailing lists. Building a mailing list is therefore the starting point for independent market-ers. Imagine you had a list of 2000 high quality pros-pects in the 'singles market?' This means a list of 2000 singles who are looking for partners. A campaign with a good product aimed at this list would give you a much bigger return on your time invested than would a random offering to the general public. In fact, 400 sales of a $20.00 product would give you $8000.00

Marketing secret 3 – Use a list-building website before using a product selling website. Do not mix the two!

The most important function of a marketing website is to capture the email addresses and first names of people who are seriously interested in your niche. Once you have a decent list, you can use emails to point them to smaller websites where goods can be purchased.

Marketing secret 4 - Treat list-building as a separate business.

You should make list building your primary business: separate to selling! This is for one simple reason; selling is simple if the list is good. This means that the selling is the easy part of your business. Building a high quality list on the other hand takes a dedicated and deliberate approach. This means creating a list building website before creating a sales-based website.

Marketing secret 5 – focus on the quality and not the quantity of your list.

A big list of disinterested people will do nothing for your business. On the other hand a small list of very interested people will work wonders for your business. Quality in a list means 3 things:

1. **Opt-in.** This means that they enter their details into a box on your website which gives you permission to send them special offers. If you simply add email addresses to your list, your emails could be considered spam. Spamming is illegal.

2. **Prospects accepting a free offer.** This could be a newsletter, a free e-book or report or a free trial period.

3. **The cap fits.** This means that your products relate directly to your prospects aspirations, fears, issues and concerns. 'It is easier to sell greasy burgers to a hungry crowd than it is to sell finer foods to a crowd of people who have just eaten!' WM

Marketing secret 6 - Use multiple websites!

There are three sorts of website:

1. **A brochure site** – this is designed to tell people who you are and what you do.

2. **A list-building site** – this is designed to capture the data of visitors. This is sometimes called a **'squeeze page!'**

3. **A sales site** – this is designed to sell products and services. It is sometimes called an e-commerce site.

Whereas you only need one brochure site, you will need to develop multiple list-building and product sales sites. It is a mistake to try and do all three from one site because it creates confusion for the consumer who is still trying to figure out what exactly you want them to do.

Marketing secret 7 – Tell your visitor what you want them to do!

Your website should clearly answer four questions for your visitor:

1. **What** exactly you want them to do. Whether it be a brochure, list or sales site; you should tell them what actions you want them to take. Do you want them to browse, subscribe or buy. There should be no confusion here.

2. **Why** it is in their own interests to do it. Your site should list the benefits of taking the actions you are prompting.

3. **How** exactly they should do what you are asking them to do.

4. **When** it should be done and of course why it should be done sooner rather than later. Timing is a big issue in consumer psychology. Put simply, if you want me to act now, then you need to give me a good reason why i.e. the offer runs out.

Chapter 12

Sales made simple

The fact is, everyone is in sales. Whatever area you work in, you do have clients and you do need to sell.

Jay Abraham

Some people fold after making one timid request. They quit too soon. Keep asking until you find the answers. In sales there are usually four or five "no's" before you get a "yes."

Jack Canfield

The ability to write persuasive copy is the master skill of smart marketers. Sales people may have the gift of the gab and can verbally persuade individuals and small groups to buy, but print masters and expert copy writers have the power to persuade people they'll never meet into buying a product online. Any amount of time or money that you invest in practising and perfecting your copy writing, will pay you untold dividends in the long run because you can reach infinitely more people in print than you can through door to door sales.

This chapter is all about the art of writing persuasive copy for your websites or promotional literature. It will explain the core components and elements of a high converting sales script. Sometimes called 'print persuasion', this science has been tried, tested and perfected over many years of trial and error. Although savvy marketers will constantly find ways to improve on this art form, it is safe to say that the core elements still work.

The anatomy of a sale

Let's start by personifying your sales copy. What I mean is, I want you to imagine that your website or brochure is a person with a head, a heart, hands, feet and a mouth. Here's why: the core components of persuasive sales copy will bring your website and other marketing documents to life and make visitors and readers feel as though they are listening to a real person.

Your sales copy needs all the components in order to bring it to life. Here they are:

The logic (head) of the sale: Buying your product must make sense (not just to you; but to the customer!). If your product doesn't address the customer's concerns, fears and pains then there is no sense in buying it. If it doesn't help them achieve their goals or realise their aspirations then the sale is illogical. The starting point then of good sales copy is to highlight the problem, the issue or the pain that people feel in that particular area of their life. This is your opportunity to quickly achieve customer rapport by empathising with them. People open up to you when they know that you understand.

The heart of the sale: Remember that a product is a means to an end. In this respect people are never buying your products; they are really buying an outcome or a result. Even if the outcome they are looking for is physical or material, the end game is always emotional. The decision to purchase is usually emotional. It is an attempt to avoid or to obtain certain feelings. Great sales copy will transport the reader into the future beyond the sale. It will get them to imagine all the things they will be able to do or the problems that they can avoid after they buy your product and will stimulate their imagination to see themselves beyond their problems and their pains. You also have to get them to see what the true price of not purchasing your product could be.

For example; if you are selling a weight loss product, then you have to give your prospects something to obtain (new image, sex appeal, confidence) and something to avoid (rejection, ill health, heart disease). You have to get them to see themselves after the weight is gone together with all the possibilities of a new slim figure.

The legs of your sale: there are two things that give your sale height and make it stand out; they are your benefits and bonuses.

- **Benefits –** As a smart marketer you must think of your products in terms of their benefits to the end user. Make a list of these benefits and make sure that they are tangible. Physical benefits and emotional benefits should be listed. Let the consumer know what they are getting and what it will do for them.

- **Bonus material –** Ensure that you add on some free bonus material for people who act swiftly. The more bonuses the better. Some of your prospects will buy your product just so they can get the bonus material. Ensure that the bonuses have real value and state what they are worth as stand alone items. (Make your bonuses digital if possible, so that you don't have the costs of fulfilment and they can be instantly downloaded. Also you should factor your bonuses into the price so that you are not out of pocket).

The hands of a sale: there are two things which grab your customer in print; they are your value to price ratio (VPR) and your limited offer.

- VPR: Your sales copy should make an irresistible offer to your prospects. Part of that is the bargain factor or the price compared to the value. You should show how much your product, together with its bonuses, are worth and then blow them away with how much it costs. As a rule you should try to create between 5 and 10 times value to price. In other words if it costs $50.00, then it should be worth between $250.00 and $500.00. Of course you need a justification for this as follows in the form of a limited offer.

- Limited offer: This may involve a time restriction or a number restriction. The offer may be for a limited time only or for a limited number of people. Another great way to create a limited offer is to sell a product review. This means that a limited number of people get to test the product at a fraction of the price.

With a product review, you may even be able to create 20 or 30 times VPR. A product worth $2900.00 may cost only $149.00 to the first 200 people as part of a product review or pre-launch test. If 200 people from your list of prospects snap it up, then you know that it can be sold for much more on the launch day! In any case you would have made a cool $29,000.00. That is a year's salary for many people.

Think about it: It's worth £2900.00 but you can have it for £149.00 as part of a prelaunch review. But you only have a one-week window to act and thereafter the offer is gone for good! These two facts, the VPR and the limited offer, literally grab your prospect and persuades them to act!

The mouth of a sale: You can amplify the voice of your sale through testimonials. Simply get three or four people to review your product and then give you some feedback. Testimonials from satisfied customers can come in written, video or audio form. You can make them more authentic by adding a photo, some contact details and making sure you have a good mix in terms of race, gender and age. (Of course this depends on the product). If the testimonials are written, then write them yourself and get the customer to sign off on them. Again, a picture and contact details will reassure prospects that these testimonials are authentic. One of the main barriers to buying is the level of risk involved. No one wants to fall prey to an internet scam or to have regrets about purchasing. Good testimonials go a long way towards assuring prospects that they are doing the right thing.

The feet of your sale: Your sales copy must promise a real relationship after the purchase. Customers must not feel as though they are on their own once they push the order button. Instead they should feel like the purchase is the beginning of a better and more meaningful relationship or that this is going somewhere good. Here are the feet of your sale:

- Guarantees: Your sales script should offer a no hassle, money back guarantee if the customer is not totally satisfied with the purchase. Of course this should be subject to terms and conditions in some cases, (i.e. physical products) but the fewer conditions the better. This can be abused, but studies have shown that the percentage of people who ask for their money back is fractional. Your guarantee should not be hidden in small print; instead it should be a very clear promise that their investment is risk free! The key to all this is that your contact details should be clearly printed in the copy.

- Support: Again, your sale has a future if a 'customer services' number or 'contact us' email address is clearly printed or promised in your sales copy. You should promise that once the purchase is made, the customer will be furnished with a special number and contact details should they need any further support!

In summary, your sales copy should and will come to life for your visitors if you:

- Quickly build rapport by identifying with the prospect's issues, concerns, fears and aspirations. This way you can ensure that the purchase makes sense.

- Promise a solution that delivers the real outcomes desired by the prospect

- Give the sale some legs with your list of benefits and bonus material. List and emphasise the benefits of the product to the end user. When you describe the product – focus on what its features mean for the customer.

- Grab the prospect with your massive value to price ratio and with the limited offer.

- Amplify the voice of your sale through testimonials

- Give your sales copy some feet or an afterlife through the promise guarantees and great customer services.

Here are a few more rules for writing effective sales letters, brochures, and web pages.

1. A logical sequence: Your words and script should follow a logical sequence by describing:

- The problems people face in this area
- Your solution
- The benefits of your solution
- The guarantees that come with your solution
- The testimonials from satisfied customers
- The Value to Price ratio (VPR)
- What action to take and how

- When to act and why (limited offer and other restrictions)
- How much they save by acting immediately

2. The human touch: People don't want to be sold at or lectured to; they want to be communicated and conversed with. The style of your copy should be conversational and relaxed. Correct English doesn't matter here. Conversational English is the key. This is an important part of achieving customer rapport. They should feel like a real person is giving them inside information on a real bargain.

Also, there is a difference between a real speech and a written one. When you listen to someone speak, they pause, speed up, slow down, emphasise words and use inflections which all aid your comprehension. In print it is difficult to do this, so you should underline, make bold, change colour or punctuate any words or phrases that you would emphasise if you were speaking. This makes the copy sound more realistic and life-like!

3. Emphasise your promise: Never forget that:

'Your promise should be bigger than your product!'

At first glance this statement can be misunderstood. It doesn't mean that you should fabricate or exaggerate the features and benefits of your product. It does mean that you should pay more attention to your promise than to the features of your product. Let me explain:

A product is a means to an end and not an end in itself. No one buys a product for the product's sake; they buy it because of what it promises to deliver. If the promise is not clear, then consumers won't buy the product.

4. Treat all stationery as a marketing tool: Even your business stationery or printed flyers should follow the above-mentioned principles. Letterheads and business cards should be treated as marketing documents. The company name or your name is important but even more important is the slogan or strap line. Your slogan should make an irresistible promise. Likewise your web address should be very visible (not small print) and people should be clearly sent to it.

Many flyers and postcards are too confusing and the design is the number one distraction. The eye simply does not know where to go because there is no logical sequence. First start with your objective: what you want them to do! If your main objective is to drive traffic to a website, then that website should be the second largest feature of your flyer. Your headline should be the most obvious feature of your flyers. Your sub headline should make an irresistible offer and your copy should achieve customer rapport by demonstrating an understanding of their issues. It should make a definite call to action and further promise a reward for those who act immediately.

Focus on the customer: The next time you look at a website, ask yourself this question; is this about them or is it about me? Most people make the mistake of designing a website that is all about themselves and their products. Smart marketers want prospects to see themselves in the website, so they make sure that their copy is totally customer focused and orientated so that it says more about the customer than it does about them.

Length: Many wonder why some sales sites are so lengthy. Here is the simple reason; because it works! The general rule is that low impact purchases require less copy, but high impact purchases ($50.00 or more) requires more proof to satisfy customer scepticisms and to address any hidden objections.

But why keep it all on the same page? Because research has shown that the more clicks a customer has to make, the less likely they are to convert. Once they get to your website, the only click they should make is the 'buy now' button!

In summary:

- Any written copy (text) should be considered a marketing document or tool.

- You should always start these documents with the end in view so that the whole document is treated as the call to a specific action. Test it when completed to see if people get the message. Tweak it until its message is clear before you launch your campaign.

- Ensure that the design of your documents does not obscure the message.

- Make sure that the eye knows where to go by making a bold headline, a smaller sub headline, easy to read fonts for the copy and a logical sequence to your argument.

- Use language that is conversational; every man's English complete with puns and jokes!

- Emphasise the words and phrases that you want to stand out in people's minds with colours, bold, italics, underline, punctuations and larger font sizes. Be sure to break up the text so that it doesn't appear like a lot to read even if it is.

- Make sure that your website is customer orientated. They don't care about you or your company, all they care about is themselves.

- If the purchase is low impact then use less copy, but if it is high impact then address any hidden objections that you can imagine. Keep it all on one page with only one place to navigate; i.e. the payment page!

Conclusion

Perhaps the most valuable result of all education is the ability to make yourself do the thing you have to do, when it ought to be done, whether you like it or not; it is the first lesson that ought to be learned; and however early a man's training begins, it is probably the last lesson that he learns thoroughly.

Thomas Henry Huxley (1825-95)
English biologist and writer.

Obviously one of my goals in writing this book is to encourage a debate about the state of education in the developed and developing worlds. I am clearly concerned about the lack of financial education, business education, leadership education and success education in schools and colleges.

I am disappointed that the very subjects that are most likely to deliver on the promise of education have been carefully omitted from the process of education. And I regret that I have had to learn in my forties what I should have learned in my teens.

However my main objective is to de-mystify success by laying certain facts on the table:

1. The majority of rich people own their own businesses while only a small minority of the world's rich have high paying jobs.

2. Owning your own business has never been more easy than it is today, particularly if you use the virtual business opportunities described in this book.

3. Making your own money is easy if you understand direct marketing and sales. You can literally sell anything to anyone, anywhere at anytime, while you sleep, using a fully automated virtual business system. You can find out more about this at www.miseducationexposed.com

4. The failure to study and understand money is a classic case of mis-education because every aspect of your adult life will be affected by it.

5. Your most valuable asset is your entrepreneurial (creative, solution-orientated) mind. A good education should both feed and encourage, ideas, imagination and initiative.

6. The doctrine of scarcity is an illusion that serves a few at the expense of the many. It is used to limit choices and to artificially inflate prices.

7. A philosophy of abundance (an attitude that says there is more than enough for everyone to have more than enough) will activate the law of recognition in your mind by highlighting the many opportunities for success, surrounding you now.

8. Re-education in the subjects that matter is the only proven road map to riches!

Now let me elaborate on this point. I have studied outstanding people in a variety of fields for over 15 years in an attempt to find out what makes them different? Here is what I discovered:

1. Each and every one of them could trace their success back to a personal turning point. This was either the point of inspiration or the point of desperation. Something brought them to the place of decision and from that moment on they had forever changed direction.

2. Each one of them came under the wings of a mentor who was able to help them in two ways: first to unlearn what they already knew and secondly to learn what they needed to know.

Put simply, 'when the student is ready, the teacher will appear!' When you have truly and finally decided to succeed; then a book, an audio, a seminar, a course, a person will appear to help you unlearn what doesn't work and to learn what does.

May this book do it for you!

Wayne

Simply
The Best
COACHING SYSTEM

A breakthrough in Personal Development

THIS PROGRAMME COMES COMPLETE WITH 16 CD'S INCLUDING:

- *12 Audio Books*

- *Transcripts*

- *Coaching Templates*

- *Over 700 articles on Personal Development*

  and more!...

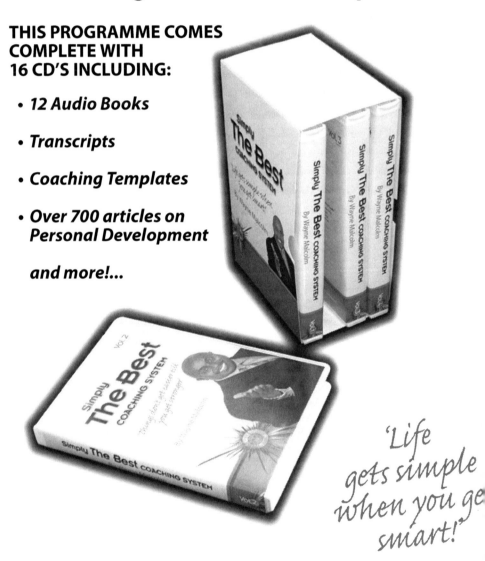

'Life gets simple when you get smart!'

Order the complete system today at
www.bestcoachingsystem.com

'Running a business from home is easy when you know how!'

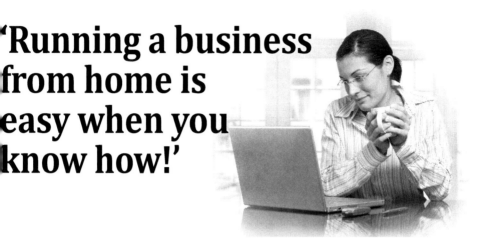

The Home business academy is an online community of ordinary individuals who are committed to creating wealth from their own home-based business. Students can select from over 50 courses covering every conceivable aspect of starting or growing a business from home. The academy comes complete with:

- **Full Tutorials,**
- **Video and audio instructions,**
- **Weekly webinars**
- **One-on-one coaching**
- **Authentic home business opportunities**

Everything you need to know in order to launch and grow your own home-based business!

To enrol now, log on to:

www.thehomebusinessacademy.com

*'There is no recession
on the world-wide web,
no recession for smart entrepreneurs
and no recession for members of the
home business academy.'*

Lightning Source UK Ltd.
Milton Keynes UK

176867UK00002B/188/P